SHIP SALE AND PURCHASE

FIRST SUPPLEMENT TO
THE SECOND EDITION

EDITOR-IN-CHIEF
IAIN S. GOLDREIN
M.A. (Cantab.) A.C.I.Arb.
Barrister, Northern Circuit
The Sir Jack Jacob Visiting Professor
of Litigation, Nottingham Law School
Companion of the British Academy of Experts

GENERAL EDITORS
JOHN BASSINDALE   PAUL TURNER
LL.B., LL.M.   M.A. (Cantab.)
Clifford Chance   *Clifford Chance*

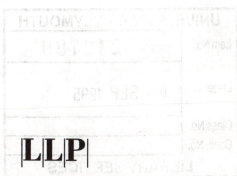

LLP

LONDON   NEW YORK   HAMBURG   HONG KONG
LLOYD'S OF LONDON PRESS LTD
1995

Lloyd's of London Press Ltd
Legal and Business Publishing Division
27 Swinton Street
London WC1X 9NW

USA AND CANADA
Lloyd's of London Press Inc.
Suite 308, 611 Broadway
New York, NY 10012 USA

GERMANY
Lloyd's of London Press GmbH
59 Ehrenbergstrasse
2000 Hamburg 50, Germany

SOUTH EAST ASIA
Lloyd's of London Press (Far East) Ltd
Room 1101, Hollywood Centre
233 Hollywood Road
Hong Kong

©
Iain S. Goldrein
1995

British Library Cataloguing in Publication Data
A catalogue record for this book is
available from the British Library

ISBN 1-85044-973-2

Text set in 10 on 12pt Times. Composed by
Lloyd's of London Press
Printed in Great Britain by
WBC Print Ltd.
Bridgend, Mid-Glamorgan

Preface

Since the second edition of *Ship Sale and Purchase* was published, there have been a number of significant developments on the subject. These include the publication of new editions of the Norwegian Saleform (code named *Saleform 1993*) and the Japanese sale terms (code named *Nipponsale 1993*), the revision of the widely used arbitration terms issued by the London Maritime Arbitrators' Association (these are known as the *LMAA Terms 1994*), and the decisions of the Court of Appeal in *The "Nicholas H"* and of the Court of Appeal and House of Lords in *The "Niobe"*.

In this Supplement we provide a clause by clause commentary on Saleform 1993, identifying the changes made from the previous form and highlighting the main differences between Saleform 1993 and Nipponsale 1993.

In the commentary on clauses 4 and 11 of Saleform 1993, we also review the decisions in *The "Nicholas H"* and *The "Niobe"*, referred to above.

Throughout, there are detailed cross-references to the second edition of *Ship Sale and Purchase* (referred to in this Supplement as the main text).

The decision of the House of Lords in *The "Niobe"* was handed down on 23 March 1995 but otherwise the law is stated, as we believe it to be, on 3 January 1995. Readers should note, however, that this Supplement is not designed to provide legal advice on specific issues or problems, in respect of which separate legal advice should be sought.

JOHN BASSINDALE
PAUL TURNER

Contents

Table of Cases

Table of United Kingdom Legislation

SECTION ONE

SALEFORM 1993

SALEFORM 1993

PREAMBLE TO SALEFORM 1993

MEMORANDUM OF AGREEMENT

Dated:

hereinafter called the Sellers, have agreed to sell, and	1
hereinafter called the Buyers, have agreed to buy	2
Name:	3
Classification Society/Class:	4
Built: By:	5
Flag: Place of Registration:	6
Call Sign: Grt/Nrt:	7
Register Number:	8
hereinafter called the Vessel, on the following terms and conditions:	9

Definitions   10

"Banking days" are days on which banks are open both in the country of the currency   11
stipulated for the Purchase Price in Clause 1 and in the place of closing stipulated in Clause 8.   12

"In writing" or "written" means a letter handed over from the Sellers to the Buyers or vice versa,   13
a registered letter, telex, telefax or other modern form of written communication.   14

"Classification Society" or "Class" means the Society referred to in line 4.   15

1. Agreement to sell

(1) Agreement to sell in future

Lines 1 and 2 have been amended so as to provide that Saleform 1993 records an agreement to sell and buy the ship at a future time rather than a sale and purchase which takes effect at the moment when the memorandum has been signed by both parties: the significance of this distinction is discussed in paragraphs 4 to 8 on pages 83–87 of the main text.

(2) When is there a binding agreement?

(a) As noted in the main text (see paragraph 3 on pages 65–71 of the main text) ship sale negotiations may be lengthy and complex, and where a party withdraws from a set of negotiations at a late stage difficult questions may arise as to whether, at the point when the party withdrew, there was a legally binding sale agreement.

(b) This question arose in *The "Gladys" (No. 2)* (1994)[1]. In that case sellers claimed damages in arbitration against Metal Scrap Trade Corporation ("MSTC") for breach of an alleged scrap sale contract. MSTC denied the existence of the sale contract and applied to the Commercial Court for a declaration that the arbitrators had no jurisdiction to hear the dispute.

(c) The Court found that, by a certain date, there was an oral agreement in relation to the sale. However, the Court decided that the oral agreement was not legally binding because it was made in terms which contemplated that there would be further negotiations about details before a binding contract could be reached.

(d) Although the Court accepted MSTC's contention that there was no legally binding agreement at the point when they withdrew from the sale negotiations, the case underlines the need for parties to keep in mind that they may become contractually bound to one another even if negotiations are continuing. If a party does not wish to be bound until all of the commercial and legal terms of the deal have been agreed and put into a written contract which has been signed by both parties, he or she should make this clear: see the commentary, at paragraph 5(5) on pages 68–71 of the main text, in relation to the use of expressions such as *"subject to details"* and *"subject to contract"*.

(e) In the course of his decision in *The "Gladys"*, the judge explained the distinction between the different broking expressions *"firm offer"* and *"sub recon offer"*. The expression *"firm offer"* means an offer firm as to price and delivery, in respect of which (once accepted) matters would speedily proceed to finalisation of the sale agreement. In contrast, the expression *"sub recon offer"* means an offer in respect of which no further negotiations would take place unless and until reconfirmed and accepted, at which stage the offer would stand on the same footing as a firm offer which had been accepted.

2. Description of the ship

(1) Alterations

The description of the ship (in lines 3 to 9) has been altered and now requires sellers to give the name of the ship's classification society, and her net and gross tonnages, as well as the other information called for by the corresponding lines in Saleform 1987.

(2) Compliance with description

(a) The vast majority of contracts for the sale of second-hand ships take effect as agreements to sell by description. This is significant because:

1. [1994] 2 Lloyd's Rep. 402.

(i) where the sale of a ship is by description the Sale of Goods Act 1979 implies a term that the ship will correspond to the description given to her in the sale contract; and

(ii) the 1979 Act categorised such an implied term as a condition, any breach of which by sellers (however minor) would give rise to a right on buyers' part to reject the ship and treat the sale contract as repudiated.

(b) This rule of strict compliance could give rise to unfairness; for example, buyers could use a minor misdescription to reject the ship in a falling market in circumstances where the resulting loss to sellers would be out of all proportion to their breach of the sale contract.

(c) This point is tackled by the Sale and Supply of Goods Act 1994 which introduces a number of amendments to the 1979 Act. The effect of section 4 of the 1994 Act is that where non-consumer (ie commercial) buyers would have had a right to reject by reason of a breach of one of the terms implied by the 1979 Act (such as the compliance with description term) but *"the breach is so slight that it would be unreasonable for [buyers] to reject [the ship] then, ... the breach is not to be treated as a breach of condition but may be treated as a breach of warranty"*.

(d) Sellers should note that:

(i) it will be for them to show that a breach passes the section 4 test; and

(ii) section 4 only applies where no contrary intention appears in, or is to be implied from, the sale contract.

(e) It is unclear precisely how the section 4 test will operate but there is obviously scope for difficulty. For example, there may be situations in which a very small deviation from a contractual description could have a significant commercial effect as far as buyers are concerned. Furthermore, what will be sufficient to indicate a *"contrary intent"* so as to exclude the new rule and to what extent can the nature of the transaction itself be taken into account in answering this question? Until the introduction of the 1994 Act (it came into force on 3 January 1995, but only in respect of contracts made after that date), buyers' right to reject for non-conformity was, if inflexible, at least clear cut. The position is now perhaps fairer but more likely to give rise to dispute.

3. New definitions

Saleform 1993 (in lines 10–15) contains new definitions of *"banking days"*, *"in writing/written"* and *"Classification Society/Class"*. The 1987 form did not have a definitions section at all, so this provision is entirely new.

4. Definition of banking days

(1) Where used

The expression *"banking days"* is used:

(a) in clause 2 of the 1993 form—buyers must pay the deposit within an agreed number of banking days from the date of the memorandum;

(b) in clause 3 of the 1993 form—buyers must pay the purchase price within three banking days after a valid notice of readiness has been given to them; and

(c) in clause 14 of the 1993 form—sellers have a maximum of 3 banking days after they have given a valid notice of readiness within which to make ready the delivery documents described in clause 8 (see page 25 below).

(2) Buyers' note

Depending on the nature of buyers' banking arrangements and the payment method to be used at completion (see paragraph 1 on pages 94–96 of the main text), buyers may wish to change the *"banking days"* definition to include days on which banks are open for business in the country in which buyers' bankers are located—that country may be different from:

(a) the country of the currency of payment under the memorandum; and

(b) the country in which the documentary completion takes place (see page 26 below).

CLAUSE 1—PURCHASE PRICE

1. Purchase Price 16

The previous distinction between *"Price"* and *"Purchase Money"* has been abandoned. Instead, the expression *"Purchase Price"* is used throughout Saleform 1993.

CLAUSE 2—DEPOSIT

2. Deposit 17

As security for the correct fulfilment of this Agreement the Buyers shall pay a deposit of 10% 18
(ten per cent) of the Purchase Price within   banking days from the date of this Agreement. This 19
deposit shall be placed with and held by them in a joint account for the Sellers and the Buyers, 20
to be released in accordance with joint written instructions of the Sellers and the Buyers. Interest, 21
if any, to be credited to the Buyers. Any fee charged for holding the said deposit shall be borne 22
equally by the Sellers and the Buyers. 23

1. Release of deposit

In this clause, new words (in lines 21 and 22) provide that the security deposit is to be released by the deposit-holding bank only against the joint written instructions of sellers and buyers. This reflects existing practice and, in any case, the new words are necessary because the deposit release language contained in clause 8 (line 92) of the 1987 form has been omitted from clause 8 of Saleform 1993.

2. Bank's mandate for joint deposit account

Since the deposit-holding bank will not be a party to the memorandum, the contracting parties (and, in particular, buyers) should ensure that the bank's mandate in relation to the joint deposit account gives effect to clause 2; it has been known for buyers to pay the security deposit to an account which is in sellers' sole name and under their exclusive control.

3. Nipponsale 1993

Clause 2(a) of the Japanese form requires buyers to establish a 10% security deposit within 3 banking days *"from the date of the Agreement"*.

CLAUSE 3—PAYMENT

3. Payment   1

The said Purchase Price shall be paid in full free of bank charges to   2
on delivery of the Vessel, but not later than 3 banking days after the Vessel is in every respect   3
physically ready for delivery in accordance with the terms and conditions of this Agreement and   4
Notice of Readiness has been given in accordance with Clause 5.   5

1. Payment without deduction

(1) New words

Clause 3 of Saleform 1987 provides that the price is to be *"paid free of bank charges ..."*. In clause 3 of Saleform 1993, at line 26, the words *"in full"* have been added after the word *"paid"*. Presumably, the purpose of this amendment is to prevent buyers from making deductions from the price on account of any claims which they may have against sellers: see paragraphs (4) and (5) on page 40, and paragraph (6) on page 96, of the main text.

(2) Sellers' note

While the new words go some way towards achieving their presumed objective, they are not as wide as the standard anti set-off formula found in many modern commercial agreements and some sellers may wish to deal with the point more comprehensively by expressly excluding all of buyers' rights of set-off and counterclaim.

2. Notice of readiness under Saleform 1987

(1) Time for payment

Clause 3 of Saleform 1987 requires the purchase money to be paid *"on delivery of the vessel, but not later than 3 banking days after the vessel is ready for delivery and written or telexed notice thereof has been given to Buyers by Sellers"*.

(2) Time for giving notice of readiness

There was some doubt, however, whether the ship had to be in a deliverable condition at the time when the notice of readiness (widely known as *"NOR"*) was given. In *The "Aktion"* (1987)[2], sellers gave NOR when the ship was at sea on her way to the delivery port and the Commercial Court held that the ship did not have to be in a deliverable condition when NOR was given, provided she was in a deliverable condition at the expiry of the notice period: see paragraph 4 on pages 97–98 in the main text.

---

2. [1987] 1 Lloyd's Rep. 283.

3. Notice of readiness under Saleform 1993

(1) The new position

(a) The 1993 form deals with the NOR issue in clauses 3, 5a) and 14 by reversing the Saleform 1987 position.

(b) The combined effect of these three provisions is that sellers may not give NOR until the ship is *"in every respect"* ready for delivery and at the place of delivery. But a distinction is drawn between the ship's *"physical"* readiness for delivery and what may be termed her legal readiness. Physical readiness must be achieved before sellers give NOR whereas legal readiness may be achieved after service of NOR but before, or upon, delivery of the ship to buyers. This means that sellers may give NOR even if they have not made ready their delivery documents (see clause 8 at page 25 below) by the time when they give NOR; lines 243 to 245 of the 1993 form (see clause 14 at page 39 below) provide that sellers are to have up to 3 banking days after NOR has been given to arrange their delivery documents.

(2) Sellers' note

The new requirement that the ship must be *"in every respect physically ready for delivery"* before sellers can give a valid NOR reflects market practice to a certain extent: see paragraph 5 on page 98 of the main text. However, some sellers may try to delete or loosen-up the requirement on the ground that, where there is a minor physical defect in the ship, the new requirement might enable unscrupulous buyers to reject, or challenge, the validity of sellers' NOR.

(3) Buyers' note

(a) Some buyers may be unwilling to go to the trouble and expense of gearing up for delivery (for example, by mobilising their crew, ordering bunkers and other consumables for the ship's post-delivery voyage, and giving a drawdown notice for an external loan) unless they are sure that the ship and her documents are ready.

(b) In practice, such buyers may try to amend the printed terms of clauses 3, 5(a) and 14 to provide that, before sellers may give a valid NOR, the ship and her documents must be in all respects physically and legally ready except in relation to specified aspects of readiness (for example, sellers' removal of items excluded from the sale or the release and deletion of any mortgages over the ship) which are to be accomplished immediately before, or upon, delivery.

4. Nipponsale 1993

(1) Payment procedure

The payment procedure set out in clause 2(b) of the Japanese form:

(a) requires buyers to pay the balance of the price to the deposit-holding bank (presumably for credit to the joint deposit account, although this is not made as clear as it could be in the Japanese form) immediately after sellers have given NOR under clause 6 of the form; and

(b) provides that the balance of the price, together with the deposit, will be released to sellers at the moment when the ship is delivered and the parties sign a protocol of delivery and acceptance.

(2) Sellers' NOR and buyers' take over of ship

Clause 7 of Nipponsale 1993 provides that:

(a) when the ship has passed the classification society drydocking inspection described in clause 6 of the form, sellers must give NOR; and

(b) buyers must take over the ship within 3 banking days of their receipt of NOR.

CLAUSE 4—INSPECTIONS

4. Inspections	30

a)* The Buyers have inspected and accepted the Vessel's classification records. The Buyers   31
  have also inspected the Vessel at/in   on   32
  and have accepted the Vessel following this inspection and the sale is outright and definite, 33
  subject only to the terms and conditions of this Agreement.   34

b)* The Buyers shall have the right to inspect the Vessel's classification records and declare   35
  whether same are accepted or not within   36

  The Sellers shall provide for inspection of the Vessel at/in   37

  The Buyers shall undertake the inspection without undue delay to the Vessel. Should the   38
  Buyers cause undue delay they shall compensate the Sellers for the losses thereby incurred.   39
  The Buyers shall inspect the Vessel without opening up and without cost to the Sellers.   40
  During the inspection, the Vessel's deck and engine log books shall be made available for   41
  examination by the Buyers. If the Vessel is accepted after such inspection, the sale shall   42
  become outright and definite, subject only to the terms and conditions of this Agreement,   43
  provided the Sellers receive written notice of acceptance from the Buyers within 72 hours   44
  after completion of such inspection.   45
  Should notice of acceptance of the Vessel's classification records and of the Vessel not be   46
  received by the Sellers as aforesaid, the deposit together with interest earned shall be   47
  released immediately to the Buyers, whereafter this Agreement shall be null and void.   48

*   *4a) and 4b) are alternatives; delete whichever is not applicable. In the absence of deletions,*   49
     alternative 4a) to apply.   50

1. Two alternatives

Clause 4 now offers two alternatives, one of which should be deleted by the parties; if the parties fail to delete one of the alternatives, they will be deemed to have chosen the first alternative (see the next following paragraph).

2. First alternative: outright sale

The first alternative (in lines 31–34) covers the outright sale situation, in which buyers have inspected and accepted the ship and her classification records during negotiations and before the Saleform contract is concluded. This is a sensible amendment since many sales are concluded on this basis: see paragraph 2 on pages 101–102 of the main text.

3. Second alternative: sale subject to inspection

(1) Three features

The second alternative (in lines 35–48) is a revised version of the inspection provision which appears in clause 4 of Saleform 1987. Even here, however, the 1993 version has three new features.

(2) Possibility of a drydock inspection

Firstly, clause 4 of Saleform 1987 provides for buyers to inspect the ship "*afloat*" but this word has been omitted from the 1993 version, leaving open the possibility of a clause 4 inspection while the ship is in drydock.

(3) Buyers' acceptance

Secondly, the period within which buyers must confirm their acceptance of the ship following inspection (line 44) has been extended from 48 to 72 hours.

(4) Release of deposit and interest

Thirdly, line 47 of the 1993 form has been amended to provide that, if buyers do not accept the ship and her classification records in time, sellers must release to buyers all of the interest which has accrued on the security deposit as well as the deposit itself. This amendment reflects market practice and clarifies a point which was not dealt with clearly in the 1987 form.

4. Scope of clause 4 inspections

(1) First stage—review of class records

A comprehensive clause 4 inspection will usually involve three distinct stages, during the first of which the surveyor will make a detailed review of the ship's class records: see paragraphs (3), (4) and (5) on pages 48–49 of the main text. Experienced surveyors generally prefer to make this review before boarding the ship because the class records may alert them to the possibility of serious problems of which they might otherwise be unaware.

(2) Second stage—inspection on board the ship

The second stage of a comprehensive clause 4 inspection will generally involve the surveyor going on board the ship and:

(a) making a close visual inspection of the ship's hull, decks, tanks, cargo spaces, accommodation, bridge and radio areas, machinery spaces, machinery and equipment;

(b) taking ultrasonic measurements of steel thicknesses, testing tank coatings, checking hatch covers and the like;

(c) reviewing the ship's deck and engine log books for recent casualties or other problems;

(d) reviewing the ship's class and trading certificates to check compliance with class and convention requirements;

(e) discussing the ship's performance, recent trading history (including types of cargo carried), and other matters relating to the ship's condition with the master and chief engineer; and

(f) making a detailed photographic record of the condition of the ship.

(3) Variable factors

In practice, the extent of any given inspection will be determined by a number of variable factors most of which will be outside the surveyor's control. These factors might include:

(a) the amount of time available for the survey (where there is a contract race in which several parties are interested in bidding for the ship, sellers may be able to impose a tight inspection timetable);

(b) the place and time at which the inspection is made (in the ideal case the surveyor would go on board in time to watch the completion of cargo discharge operations, after which he would have free access to the ship's empty cargo spaces);

(c) the degree of co-operation extended by the master and crew; and

(d) the state of the sea and weather during the inspection.

(4) Third stage—the report

The third stage of a comprehensive clause 4 inspection is the reporting stage. In many cases surveyors report back to buyers (by telephone, telex or fax) and discuss the survey strategy during the course of the on-board inspection. However, immediately after the inspection has been completed, many surveyors also prepare a detailed written report which:

(a) records where and when the inspection was made;

(b) describes the ship's main technical particulars and dimensions;

(c) outlines the ship's classification details and her class survey status (items which are overdue or due in the next 3 to 6 months would usually be noted);

(d) reviews the ship's trading certificates;

(e) describes the ship's machinery and equipment;

(f) includes any relevant entries from the ship's logs;

(g) contains a detailed report of the conditions found on board the ship and the surveyor's observations upon, and conclusions in relation to, those conditions and the ship; and

(h) contains a detailed and indexed photographic record (which will often be made up of a combination of video film and close-up stills) of the ship.

(5) Length of clause 4 inspections

It can be seen that clause 4 inspections may be both comprehensive and time consuming. For example the inspection of a capesize bulk carrier and her class records could take about six working days:

(a) depending on the age of the ship, the class record review could occupy the best part of one day;

(b) depending on the age and size of the ship (and the variable factors noted in paragraph 4(3) above), the on-board inspection could take up to four full working days; and

(c) the surveyor could spend at least one more full working day pulling together his conclusions and preparing the written inspection report.

5. *Buyers' notes*

(1) **Post-contract inspections**

Where buyers have made a cursory inspection of the ship and her class records during the pre-contract negotiations and wish to make a more detailed inspection after the contract has been concluded, they must make their choice clear by deleting the outright sale alternative in lines 35–48; if they fail to do this, the outright sale alternative will apply automatically.

(2) **Insurance surveys**

If buyers wish to have the right to:

(a) arrange for a condition survey[3] to be made by insurance surveyors; and

(b) reject the ship and withdraw from the contract without liability on their part in the event of the ship failing to pass such a survey,

buyers should negotiate for an appropriate amendment to the printed terms of clause 4: see paragraph (6) on pages 175–176 in the main text.

6. *Buyers' reliance on class records*

(1) **The debate**

There is a continuing debate as to whether buyers should be able to bring a claim against a ship's classification society where the society's certification of the ship is flawed in some way and, in consequence of their reliance on the flawed certification, buyers suffer a foreseeable loss: see The *"Morning Watch"* (1990),[4] discussed at paragraph (3) on pages 102–103 of the main text.

(2) **The "Nicholas H"**

(a) In a somewhat different context, in The *"Nicholas H"* (1992)[5] (see paragraph 3 (6) on page 104 of the main text) the Commercial Court decided that a classification society could owe a duty of care to cargo owners which was capable of giving rise to a liability in damages for the society's negligent certification of the ship.

(b) However, the Court of Appeal allowed the appeal made by the classification

---

3. The Salvage Association has, for many years, carried out condition surveys of ships on behalf of the London Insurance Market. These include the surveys conducted on behalf of the Joint Hull Committee of the Institute of London Underwriters known as "*JH 115A*" (the Salvage Association's standard condition survey) and "*JH 722*" (the more searching structural condition survey).

4. [1990] 1 Lloyd's Rep. 547.

5. [1992] 2 Lloyd's Rep. 481.

society.[6] The Court of Appeal's decision had three limbs.

   (i) First, the Court held that whatever the loss suffered by the claimant (whether it was physical loss or financial loss), it was necessary for the claimant to prove that (1) the loss was foreseeable, (2) there was a sufficiently close relationship between the parties, and (3) in all the circumstances it was fair, just and reasonable to impose a duty of care on the classification society.

   (ii) Secondly, the Court rejected cargo owners' argument that as the ship owners owed a duty to cargo to use due diligence to make the ship seaworthy before and at the beginning of the voyage, so the classification society must owe an identical duty to cargo owners. The Court rejected this argument because, while the ship owners' duty to cargo was qualified by the balancing factors (including limitations on the amount of damages recoverable, time bars and strict evidential provisions) contained in the Hague Rules (which were incorporated into the bills of lading under which the cargo was carried), the classification society's duty (as proposed by cargo owners) would not have been qualified by those internationally recognised and accepted balancing factors. It followed, and the Court of Appeal held, that cargo owners' proposition was not fair, just or reasonable.

   (iii) Thirdly, in the circumstances of the case, there was no relationship which could support the existence of a duty of care owed by the classification society to the cargo owners nor would it be fair, just or reasonable to impose such a duty on the classification society.

   (c) This means that, for the time being, The "Morning Watch" (1990) continues to be the leading case about the nature (and limitations) of the relationship between a ship's classification society and buyers of the ship.

7. Nipponsale 1993

The preamble to the Japanese form states that buyers have inspected and accepted the ship and her classification records before the Nipponsale contract is concluded.

CLAUSE 5—NOTICES, TIME AND PLACE OF DELIVERY

5. Notices, time and place of delivery	51
a) The Sellers shall keep the Buyers well informed of the Vessel's itinerary and shall	52
provide the Buyers with , , and days notice of the estimated time of arrival at the	53
intended place of drydocking/underwater inspection/delivery. When the Vessel is at the place	54
of delivery and in every respect physically ready for delivery in accordance with this	55
Agreement, the Sellers shall give the Buyers a written Notice of Readiness for delivery.	56
b) The Vessel shall be delivered and taken over safely afloat at a safe and accessible berth or	57
anchorage at/in	58

---

6. [1994] 1 Lloyd's Rep. 487.

in the Sellers' option.   59

Expected time of delivery: 60

Date of cancelling (see Clauses 5c), 6b) (iii) and 14):   61

c) If the Sellers anticipate that, notwithstanding the exercise of due diligence by them, the   62
   Vessel will not be ready for delivery by the cancelling date they may notify the Buyers in   63
   writing stating the date when they anticipate that the Vessel will be ready for delivery and   64
   propose a new cancelling date. Upon receipt of such notification the Buyers shall have the   65
   option of either cancelling this Agreement in accordance with Clause 14 within 7 running   66
   days of receipt of the notice or of accepting the new date as the new cancelling date. If the   67
   Buyers have not declared their option within 7 running days of receipt of the Sellers'   68
   notification or if the Buyers accept the new date, the date proposed in the Sellers' notification 69
   shall be deemed to be the new cancelling date and shall be substituted for the cancelling   70
   date stipulated in line 61.   71

   If this Agreement is maintained with the new cancelling date all other terms and conditions   72
   hereof including those contained in Clauses 5a) and 5c) shall remain unaltered and in full   73
   force and effect. Cancellation or failure to cancel shall be entirely without prejudice to any   74
   claim for damages the Buyers may have under Clause 14 for the Vessel not being ready by   75
   the original cancelling date.   76

d) Should the Vessel become an actual, constructive or compromised total loss before delivery   77
   the deposit together with interest earned shall be released immediately to the Buyers   78
   whereafter this Agreement shall be null and void.   79

1. Notices

(1) Advance notices and NOR

Clause 5a) in Saleform 1993 requires sellers to give three notices (the length of each of which is to be agreed between the parties and inserted in line 53 of the memorandum) of the ship's estimated time of arrival at the intended place of drydocking/underwater inspection/delivery (this reflects market practice: see paragraph 5 on page 107 of the main text). There is then the provision, referred to at paragraph 3(1) on page 8 above, for the giving of a written NOR once she is there.

2. Place of delivery

(1) Delivery range

Clause 5 b) of Saleform 1993 provides for the parties to agree (and insert in the space in line 58) a defined geographical delivery range. This reflects market practice: see paragraph 2(1) on page 105 of the main text.

(2) Safety requirement for the place of delivery

Clause 5b) of the 1993 form contains new words (in lines 57–58) requiring sellers to deliver the ship *"safely afloat at a safe and accessible berth or anchorage"*. Again, this change reflects market practice: see paragraph 2(1) on page 105 of the main text.

3. Cancelling date

(1) Passing of cancelling date

At clause 5b), line 61 there is a space for the agreed cancelling date to be inserted. The passing of this date may trigger buyers' right to claim compensation and/or cancel the contract under the sellers' default clause (see clause 14 at page 39 below). This, in itself, is not a new provision.

(2) New cancelling date

Clause 5c) does, however, introduce a new provision under which sellers may propose a new cancelling date if, despite due diligence on their part, they anticipate that the ship will not be ready for delivery by the original cancelling date. This new provision reflects the transfer to the sale and purchase market of a contractual device which is relatively common in the chartering market: see paragraph 4(2) on pages 106–107 of the main text.

(3) Buyers' choice

If sellers propose a new cancelling date, buyers have a choice:

(a) they may cancel the contract within seven running days of receipt of sellers' notice, recover the deposit and all accrued interest, and (if they have incurred losses which are due to sellers' proven negligence) claim compensation from sellers under clause 14; or

(b) alternatively, buyers may accept the new cancelling date without prejudice to any claim for damages which they may have under clause 14 on account of sellers' failure to make the ship ready by the original cancelling date.

(4) Time limit for buyers' response

Buyers should note that if they do not respond to sellers' notice within seven running days of receipt, the date proposed by sellers in their notice will automatically become the new cancelling date under the contract.

(5) Purpose of new cancelling date provision

The purpose of clause 5c) is to lay down a specific procedure for amending the cancelling date but, save as noted at paragraph 3(4) above, the clause does not appear significantly to alter the position which would obtain without clause 5c).

4. Constructive total loss before delivery

(1) Saleform 1987

Clause 5 of the 1987 form provides for the contract to be *"null and void"* if the ship becomes a total or constructive total loss before delivery.

(2) Saleform 1993

Clause 5d) of the 1993 form widens the application of this rule by introducing a reference to the "*compromised*" total loss of the ship.

(3) Compromised total loss

A compromised total loss may be said to occur where there is neither an actual total loss nor a constructive total loss of the ship, but the estimated value of the ship if repaired does not justify the projected repair costs, and underwriters therefore agree to a compromised settlement for the total loss of the ship: see paragraph 6 on pages 107–108 in the main text.

(4) Return of deposit and interest

Clause 5d) has also been amended to provide that, if the Saleform contract does become null and void, buyers are entitled to recover all of the interest which has accrued on the security deposit as well as the deposit itself. This amendment reflects market practice and clarifies a point which was not dealt with clearly in the 1987 form—see paragraph 6(1) on page 107 of the main text.

(5) Sellers' note

Clause 5d) is presumably intended to preclude a claim for damages by buyers, even if the loss of the ship was caused by sellers' fault, but it does not say so expressly and sellers sometimes seek to clarify this point by a short negotiated amendment to the printed terms of the clause.

5. *Nipponsale 1993*

(1) Notice provisions

Under clause 4(c) of the Japanese form, sellers must keep buyers informed of the ship's delivery and give buyers 30/15/7/3 days notice of "*approximate expected place and date of readiness for delivery*".

(2) Delivery provisions

The delivery provisions in clause 4(b) of the Japanese form provide that:

(a) if sellers fail to make the ship "*ready for delivery*" on or before the contractual cancelling date, buyers have the option of maintaining or cancelling the contract and must declare this option within 48 hours (Saturdays, Sundays and holidays excepted) from the cancelling date; and

(b) sellers will be excused (and buyers must, therefore, accept) any delay in delivery of up to 30 days provided that the delay is caused by:

(i) *force majeure* (see paragraph 2 below); and/or

(ii) repairs required to enable the ship to pass the pre-delivery classification society drydocking inspection described in clause 6 of Nipponsale 1993.

(3) *Force majeure* in Nipponsale 1993

Clause 8 of Nipponsale 1993 provides that if:

(a) the ship becomes an actual or constructive total loss before delivery, or

(b) it is not possible for her to be delivered as a result of the *"outbreak of war, political reasons, restraint of Governments, Princes or People, or any other cause which either party cannot prevent"*,

the contract will be null and void and the deposit shall at once be returned to buyers—presumably with accrued interest (which belongs to buyers under clause 2), although this point is not expressly covered in clause 8 of the Japanese form.

(3) Application of frustration and *force majeure* to Saleform 1993

(a) Unlike the Japanese form, Saleform 1993 does not contain a *force majeure* provision.

(b) The expression *"force majeure"* has no defined meaning in English law (see paragraph (5)(a) on page 31 of the main text) and if the parties to a Saleform contract wish to provide for force majeure, they must negotiate and include an additional clause which clearly defines what is meant by force majeure and how the force majeure provision is to operate.

(c) In the absence of an additional force majeure clause, Saleform contracts which are governed by English law will still be subject to the doctrine of frustration. It is beyond the scope of this Supplement to consider the frustration doctrine in detail[7] but the classic definition of frustration was framed by Lord Radcliffe in *Davis Contractors Ltd.* v. *Fareham U.D.C.* (1956)[8]:

... frustration occurs whenever the law recognises that without default of either party a contractual obligation has become incapable of being performed because the circumstances in which performance is called for would render it a thing radically different from that which was undertaken by the contract ... It was not this that I promised to do ... There must be such a change in the significance of the obligation that the thing undertaken would, if performed, be a different thing from that contracted for ...

(d) Sellers and buyers should note that frustration is a concept of narrow scope. It does not apply merely because the market conditions have changed radically since the making of the contract, or because it would be unfair in the changed circumstances to hold one or other of the parties to the strict terms of the contract. Thus, if a party is still able to perform its contractual obligations albeit with additional costs or subject to a considerable delay then, generally, there will be no frustration.

(e) In broad terms, the doctrine of frustration is limited to circumstances where performance of the contract has become physically impossible (e.g., through loss of the ship—see lines 77 to 79 in clause 5d)) of the 1993 form at page 14 above) or illegal or otherwise radically different. Furthermore, where the doctrine of frustration applies, it will generally operate to release the parties from further performance of their contractual obligations and to discharge the frustrated contract; unlike some *force majeure* provisions, the doctrine will not allow the parties' contractual obligations to be modified in any way.

7. See the standard contract texts: *Chitty on Contracts* (Twenty-seventh Edition), and *Benjamin's Sale of Goods* (Fourth Edition).
8. [1956] A.C. 696, 739.

CLAUSE 6—DRYDOCKING/DIVERS INSPECTION

6. Drydocking/Divers inspection   80

a)** The Sellers shall place the Vessel in drydock at the port of delivery for inspection by the   81
      Classification Society of the Vessel's underwater parts below the deepest load line, the   82
      extent of the inspection being in accordance with the Classification Society's rules. If the   83
      rudder, propeller, bottom or other underwater parts below the deepest load line are found   84
      broken, damaged or defective so as to affect the Vessel's class, such defects shall be made   85
      good at the Sellers' expense to the satisfaction of the Classification Society without   86
      condition/recommendation.*   87

b)** (i) The Vessel is to be delivered without drydocking. However, the Buyers shall   88
      have the right at their expense to arrange for an underwater inspection by a diver approved   89
      by the Classification Society prior to the delivery of the Vessel. The Sellers shall at their   90
      cost make the Vessel available for such inspection. The extent of the inspection and the   91
      conditions under which it is performed shall be to the satisfaction of the Classification   92
      Society. If the conditions at the port of delivery are unsuitable for such inspection, the   93
      Sellers shall make the Vessel available at a suitable alternative place near to the delivery   94
      port.   95

      (ii) If the rudder, propeller, bottom or other underwater parts below the deepest load line   96
      are found broken, damaged or defective so as to affect the Vessel's class, then unless   97
      repairs can be carried out afloat to the satisfaction of the Classification Society, the Sellers 98
      shall arrange for the Vessel to be drydocked at their expense for inspection by the   99
      Classification Society of the Vessel's underwater parts below the deepest load line, the   100
      extent of the inspection being in accordance with the Classification Society's rules. If the   101
      rudder, propeller, bottom or other underwater parts below the deepest load line are found   102
      broken, damaged or defective so as to affect the Vessel's class, such defects shall be made   103
      good by the Sellers at their expense to the satisfaction of the Classification Society   104
      without condition/recommendation.* In such event the Sellers are to pay also for the cost of   105
      the underwater inspection and the Classification Society's attendance.   106

      (iii) If the Vessel is to be drydocked pursuant to Clause 6b) (ii) and no suitable dry-   107
      docking facilities are available at the port of delivery, the Sellers shall take the Vessel   108
      to a port where suitable drydocking facilities are available, whether within or outside the   109
      delivery range as per Clause 5b). Once drydocking has taken place the Sellers shall deliver   110
      the Vessel at a port within the delivery range as per Clause 5b) which shall, for the   111
      purpose of this Clause, become the new port of delivery. In such event the cancelling date   112
      provided for in Clause 5b) shall be extended by the additional time required   113
      for the drydocking and extra steaming, but limited to a maximum of 14 running days.   114

c)   If the Vessel is drydocked pursuant to Clause 6a) or 6b) above   115

      (i) the Classification Society may require survey of the tailshaft system, the extent of   116
      the survey being to the satisfaction of the Classification surveyor. If such survey is not   117
      required by the Classification Society, the Buyers shall have the right to require the tailshaft 118
      to be drawn and surveyed by the Classification Society, the extent of the survey being in   119
      accordance with the Classification Society rules for tailshaft survey and consistent with   120
      the current stage of the Vessel's survey cycle. The Buyers shall declare whether they   121
      require the tailshaft to be drawn and surveyed not later than by the completion of the   122
      inspection by the Classification Society. The drawing and refitting of the tailshaft shall be   123
      arranged by the Sellers. Should any parts of the tailshaft system be condemned or found   124
      defective so as to affect the Vessel's class, those parts shall be renewed or made good at   125
      the Sellers' expense to the satisfaction of the Classification Society without   126
      condition/recommendation.*   127

      (ii) the expenses relating to the survey of the tailshaft system shall be borne   128
      by the Buyers unless the Classification Society requires such survey to be carried out, in   129
      which case the Sellers shall pay these expenses. The Sellers shall also pay the expenses   130
      if the Buyers require the survey and parts of the system are condemned or found defective   131
      or broken so as to affect the Vessel's class.*   132

(iii) the expenses in connection with putting the Vessel in and taking her out of   133
drydock, including the drydock dues and the Classification Society's fees shall be paid by   134
the Sellers if the Classification Society issues any condition/recommendation* as a result   135
of the survey or if it requires survey of the tailshaft system. In all other cases the Buyers   136
shall pay the aforesaid expenses, dues and fees.   137

(iv) the Buyers' representative shall have the right to be present in the drydock, but   138
without interfering with the work or decisions of the Classification surveyor.   139

(v) the Buyers shall have the right to have the underwater parts of the Vessel   140
cleaned and painted at their risk and expense without interfering with the Sellers' or the   141
Classification surveyor's work, if any, and without affecting the Vessel's timely delivery. If,   142
however, the Buyers' work in drydock is still in progress when the Sellers have   143
completed the work which the Sellers are required to do, the additional docking time   144
needed to complete the Buyers' work shall be for the Buyers' risk and expense. In the event   145
that the Buyers' work requires such additional time, the Sellers may upon completion of the   146
Sellers' work tender Notice of Readiness for delivery whilst the Vessel is still in drydock   147
and the Buyers shall be obliged to take delivery in accordance with Clause 3, whether   148
the Vessel is in drydock or not and irrespective of Clause 5b).   149

*   Notes, if any, in the surveyor's report which are accepted by the Classification Society   150
without condition/recommendation are not to be taken into account.   151

**   *6a) and 6b) are alternatives; delete whichever is not applicable. In the absence of deletions,*   152
alternative 6a) to apply.   153

1. First part of new regime

(1) Choice of inspection procedures

Clause 6 of Saleform 1993 contains a new three part regime, the first part of which
—in clauses 6a) and 6b)—contains a choice of two alternative inspection procedures.

(2) First alternative: drydocking inspection

(a) The first alternative (in lines 81–87) provides for a surveyor of the ship's classification society to carry out a pre-delivery drydocking inspection of the ship's
underwater parts. These are now defined as the parts below her deepest load line
whereas in clause 6 of the 1987 form the bottom survey is of the parts below the
ship's summer load line.

(b) The extent of the drydocking inspection will be determined by the classification society's rules.

(c) If any of the ship's underwater parts are found to be broken, damaged or
defective so as to affect the ship's class, the relevant parts must be made good at sellers' expense to the satisfaction of class without condition or recommendation.

(2) Second alternative: divers inspection

(a) The second alternative (in lines 88–114) lays down a new procedure under
which buyers may (at their expense) arrange a pre-delivery inspection of the ship's

underwater parts by a class approved diver. Sellers (at their expense) are to make the ship available for the diver's inspection and, if conditions at the port of delivery are unsuitable for such an inspection, sellers are to make the ship available at a suitable alternative plave near to the delivery port. The inclusion of this option reflects market practice to a certain extent: see paragraph 4 on page 115, and paragraph 2 on page 171, of the main text. However, there does not appear to be any generally accepted diver's inspection clause in the second-tonnage market and it is therefore likely that, in many cases, the printed terms of clause 6b) will be modified by negotiated amendments.

(b) The extent of the diver's inspection, as well as actual implementation and supervision of the inspection, is left to the ship's classification society.

(c) If the diver's inspection reveals that the rudder, propeller, bottom or other underwater parts below the ship's deepest load line are broken, damaged or defective so as to affect the ship's class and the damage cannot be repaired afloat to the satisfaction of class, sellers must arrange for the ship to be drydocked at their expense (but see paragraph 2(3) on page 21 below) for a further class inspection.

(d) If that drydock inspection confirms the presence of bottom damage affecting the ship's class, sellers must repair the damage at their expense to the satisfaction of class, and pick up the costs of the diver's inspection as well as the costs of the class surveyor's attendance.

(e) Where sellers are obliged to drydock the ship following the diver's inspection but no suitable drydocking facilities are available at the port of delivery, two backstop provisions come into play:

(i) the first provision (in lines 107–112) enables sellers to take the ship to a suitable drydock (within or outside the contractual delivery range) and, after completion of the drydocking and any necessary repairs, to tender the ship for delivery at any suitable port within the contractual delivery range; and

(ii) the second provision (in lines 112–114) automatically extends the contractual cancelling date by the additional time which sellers require in order to complete the drydocking operation and tender the ship for delivery—but sellers should note that automatic extension is subject to a cap of 14 running days.

2. Second part of new regime

(1) Scope and application

The second part of the new regime—which is set out in clause 6c) (i) to (iv) of the 1993 form—contains provisions dealing with the survey of the ship's tailshaft system, the allocation of responsibility for the costs of the drydocking and survey operations, and buyers' attendance during drydocking. These provisions apply where the ship is drydocked under clause 6a) or 6b) of the 1993 form.

(2) Tailshaft survey

(a) The tailshaft survey wording in clause 6c) divides into five parts, the first of which (in lines 116–117) provides that the class society may require a survey of the tailshaft system. The extent of the survey will be determined by the class surveyor on the spot but buyers should note that such a survey would not necessarily involve the drawing of the tailshaft.

(b) The second part of the tailshaft survey wording (in lines 117–121) provides that, if class do not require a survey of the tailshaft system, buyers may require the tailshaft to be drawn and surveyed by class. The extent of this survey will depend upon the particular class society's rules for tailshaft surveys and upon the current stage of the ship's survey cycle. Buyers should note that this survey would not necessarily involve class inspecting the whole of the ship's tailshaft system; if buyers wish to have the right to require a class survey of the entire tailshaft system they should negotiate for an appropriate amendment to the printed terms of clause 6c)(i).

(c) The third part of the clause 6c) wording states (in lines 121–123) that, if buyers wish sellers to arrange for the tailshaft to be drawn, buyers must request this, at the latest, by completion of the class inspection of the ship in the drydock.

(d) Fourthly, if any parts of the tailshaft system are condemned or found to be defective so as to affect the ship's class, the relevant parts must be renewed or made good at sellers' expense to the satisfaction of class without condition or recommendation (see lines 124–127).

(e) Fifthly, the new tailshaft survey provisions state (in lines 128–132) that the expenses relating to the tailshaft survey are to be paid by buyers unless:

  (i) class requires the tailshaft system survey to be carried out, or

  (ii) buyers require the tailshaft to be drawn and parts of the system are condemned or found to be defective or broken so as to affect the ship's class,

in which case sellers must pay the relevant expenses.

(3) Responsibility for drydocking costs

(a) Clause 6c)(iii) of the 1993 form provides that the expenses of putting the ship in and taking her out of the drydock (which are expressed to include drydock dues and class society fees—in the 1987 form the corresponding reference is to drydock costs and surveyor's fees) are to be paid by buyers unless:

  (i) class imposes any condition or recommendation as a result of the drydock inspection, or

  (ii) class requires a tailshaft system survey,

in which case sellers must pay the relevant expenses.

(b) There is a conflict between lines 133–137 in clause 6c)(iii) and lines 96–101 in clause 6b)(ii). Lines 96–101 provide that sellers will be responsible for the costs of putting the ship in and taking her out of drydock (including drydock dues) irrespective of whether or not the drydock inspection confirms the existence of bottom damage affecting the ship's class. Line 115 provides that clause 6c) applies where the ship is drydocked under either clause 6a) or clause 6b) but if lines 133–137 are intenbde to override lines 96–101, this could have been more clearly stated. In the circumstances, sellers may wish to clarify the point be negotiating for an appropriate amendment to the printed terms of clause 6c).

(c) The position under clause 6 of the 1987 form (see paragraph (6) on page 112 of the main text) is that buyers are responsible for the drydock unless:

(i)   the drydock inspection discloses damage to the ship's underwater parts which is such as to affect the her clean certificate of class; or

(ii) class requires the tailshaft to be drawn.

(4) Buyers' attendance on the drydocking inspection

(a) Clause 6c)(iv) of the 1993 form allows buyers to be represented in the drydock during the class inspection provided that buyers' representative does not interfere with the work or the decision of the class surveyor.

(b) The insertion of the reference to the surveyor's "*work*" makes the proviso to this clause slightly wider than the corresponding proviso in the 1987 form—see paragraph (5) on page 113 of the main text.

3. *Third part of new regime*

(1) Buyers' drydock works

The third part of the new regime (in clause 6c) (v) of the 1993 form) contains provisions enabling buyers to clean and paint the ship's underwater parts while she is in drydock, provided that these works do not delay delivery of the ship or interfere with the work of sellers or the class surveyor. This change reflects market practice: see paragraph 2(3) on page 113 in the main text.

(2) Delivery in the drydock

If buyers' drydock works are continuing at the time when the ship is ready for delivery at a drydock, sellers will be released from their obligation to deliver the ship afloat (see line 57 in clause 5b) at page 13 above) with the result that they may give NOR and deliver the ship to buyers while she is in the drydock. However, it is not clear whether sellers would be entitled to rely on this provision where they have taken the ship to a drydock outside the contractual delivery range (see paragraph 1(2)(e) on page 21 above). If sellers wish to make it clear that they can deliver in a drydock outside the contractual delivery range in such circumstances, it may be better for them to negotiate for an appropriate amendment to the printed terms of clause 6c)(v).

4. *Sellers' notes*

(a) Sellers should note that if they wish to deliver the ship on the basis of a diver's inspection only, they must make their choice clear by deleting the drydocking alternative in lines 81–87; if they fail to do this, the drydocking alternative will apply automatically.

(b) Sellers should also note that the cancelling date extension mechanism provided for in lines 112–114 of clause 6b)(iii) is not expressed to apply where conditions at the delivery port are not suitable for a diver's inspection and sellers are required (under lines 93–95 of clause 6b)(i)) to make the ship available for a diver's inspection at a suitable alternative place near to the delivery port—some sellers may wish to cover this point by a negotiation amended to the printed terms of clause 6b).

5. *Buyers' notes*

(a) In clause 6 of the 1993 form the requirement that sellers are to make good breakages, damages or defects affecting the ship's class could be more favourable to buyers than the references in clause 6 of the 1987 form which requires sellers to remedy breakages, damages or defects affecting the ship's "*clean certificate of class*".

(b) Where sellers intend to deliver the ship while she is in drydock (see paragraph 3(2) above), buyers would be well advised to make sure that there is no risk of the yard asserting a possessory lien over the ship in respect of sellers' pre-delivery works: see paragraph (2) on pages 105 and 106 of the main text.

6. *Nipponsale 1993*

(1) Drydocking requirement

Clause 6 of the Japanese form requires sellers to place the ship into drydock "*at the port of delivery or near thereto prior to delivery*" for:

(a) a classification society drydocking inspection of the ship's bottom and underwater parts below the summer load line; and

(b) if buyers (or the class surveyor) should so require, the drawing and inspection of the ship's tailshaft.

(2) Defects found

If the ship's underwater parts, or (if drawn) the tailshaft, are found to be broken or damaged or defective so as to affect the ship's clean certificate of class, the relevant parts must be renewed or made good at sellers' expense to class satisfaction without qualification.

(3) Responsibility for costs

(a) Save as provided in paragraph (b) below, buyers must pay:

    (i) the expenses of putting the ship into and taking her out of the drydock;

    (ii) the drydock dues and class surveyor's fees; and

    (iii) the costs of drawing the tailshaft.

(b) However, if:

    (i) the class surveyor requires the tailshaft to be drawn, made good or renewed, or

    (ii) the ship's underwater parts are found to be broken, damaged or defective so as to affect the ship's clean certificate of class,

sellers must pay the expenses, dues, fees and costs referred to in paragraph (a) above.

(c) In any event, sellers must pay all costs of bringing the ship to the drydock and from the drydock to the contractual place of delivery.

CLAUSE 7—SPARES/BUNKERS

7. Spares/bunkers, etc.   154

The Sellers shall deliver the Vessel to the Buyers with everything belonging to her on board and on   155
shore. All spare parts and spare equipment including spare tail-end shaft(s) and/or spare   156
propeller(s)/propeller blade(s), if any, belonging to the Vessel at the time of inspection used or   157
unused, whether on board or not shall become the Buyers' property, but spares on order are to be   158
excluded. Forwarding charges, if any, shall be for the Buyers' account. The Sellers are not required to   159
replace spare parts including spare tail-end shaft(s) and spare propeller(s)/propeller blade(s) which   160
are taken out of spare and used as replacement prior to delivery, but the replaced items shall be the   161
property of the Buyers. The radio installation and navigational equipment shall be   162
included in the sale without extra payment if they are the property of the Sellers. Unused stores and
provisions shall be   163
included in the sale and be taken over by the Buyers without extra payment.   164

The Sellers have the right to take ashore crockery, plates, cutlery, linen and other articles bearing the   165
Sellers' flag or name, provided they replace same with similar unmarked items. Library, forms, etc.,   166
exclusively for use in the Sellers' vessel(s), shall be excluded without compensation. Captain's,   167
Officers' and Crew's personal belongings including the slop chest are to be excluded from the sale,   168
as well as the following additional items (including items on hire):   169

The Buyers shall take over the remaining bunkers and unused lubricating oils in storage tanks and sealed
drums and pay the   170
current net market price (excluding barging expenses) at the port and date   171
of delivery of the Vessel.   172
Payment under this Clause shall be made at the same time and place and in the same currency as   173
the Purchase Price.   174

1. Spares

In clause 7 of the 1993 form the description of the spare parts and spare equipment to be delivered with the ship (lines 157 to 160) has been widened to include spare propeller blade(s), if any.

2. Unused stores and provisions

(1) Saleform 1987

Under the 1987 form, unused stores and provisions must be taken over and paid for by buyers on delivery.

(2) Saleform 1993

Lines 163 and 164 of the 1993 form reverse this position by providing that unused stores and provisions are included in the sale without charge to buyers. This change reflects market practice but where the ship's unused stores and provisions are of high value (for example, in a cruise or ferry sale), sellers may negotiate for a term obliging buyers to pay an agreed price for these items or permitting sellers to remove such items from the ship before delivery.

3. Items on hire

(a) A new reference (in line 169 of the 1993 form) to items on hire makes it clear that such items are excluded from the sale.

(b) However, where appropriate and practicable (bearing in mind that usually it will be necessary to clear a transfer with the owner of the hired items), the parties may agree to amend the sale contract so as to provide that buyers will take over the relevant hire contracts with effect from delivery of the ship.

4. Inventory and excluded items

(1) Good practice

Before the sale terms are finally agreed, the parties would be well advised jointly to draw up and agree:
    (a) an inventory of the ship's equipment; and
    (b) a list of the items which are to be excluded from the sale.

(2) Excluded items list

The excluded items list should clearly identify all items which are not owned by sellers (unless, by prior arrangement with the legal owner of those items, buyers will assume sellers' hire/lease/licence/rental obligations on delivery of the ship), as well as any other items which sellers own but wish to exclude from the sale.

5. Price of bunkers and unused lubricating oils

(1) The argument

Sellers sometimes angle for a gross price (which may include barging costs but exclude any discounts or rebates allowed to sellers) whereas buyers usually prefer to pay a net price: see paragraph 7(2) on page 119 of the main text.

(2) The Saleform 1993 formula

The formula used in lines 170 to 172 of the 1993 form comes down on buyers' side of the argument by requiring them to pay for bunkers and unused lubricating oils at the current net market price (excluding barging expenses) at the port and date of delivery of the ship; unused lubricating oils are now described as unused oils in storage tanks and sealed drums.

(3) Buyers' note

In practice, some buyers may still negotiate for an amendment which aims to:
    (a) lay down minimum/maximum delivery balances; and
    (b) fix the price by reference to sellers' properly documented last paid net prices, excluding barging expenses and including any applicable discounts or rebates.

6. Nipponsale 1993

Clause 10 of the Japanese form requires buyers to take over and pay for sellers' remaining bunkers and unused lubricating oils at the "*last purchased prices evidenced by supporting vouchers*".

CLAUSE 8—DOCUMENTATION

8. Documentation	175
The place of closing:	176
In exchange for payment of the Purchase Price the Sellers shall furnish the Buyers with delivery documents, namely:	177 178

a) Legal Bill of Sale in a form recordable in   (the country in which the Buyers are   179
   to register the Vessel), warranting that the Vessel is free from all encumbrances, mortgages   180
   and maritime liens or any other debts or claims whatsoever, duly notarially attested and   181

   legalised by the consul of such country or other competent authority.   182
b) Current Certificate of Ownership issued by the competent authorities of the flag state of   183
   the Vessel.   184

c) Confirmation of Class issued within 72 hours prior to delivery.   185

d) Current Certificate issued by the competent authorities stating that the Vessel is free from   186
   registered encumbrances.   187

e) Certificate of Deletion of the Vessel from the Vessel's registry or other official evidence of 188
   deletion appropriate to the Vessel's registry at the time of delivery, or, in the event that the 189
   registry does not as a matter of practice issue such documentation immediately, a written   190
   undertaking by the Sellers to effect deletion from the Vessel's registry forthwith and furnish 191
   a Certificate or other official evidence of deletion to the Buyers promptly and latest within 4 192
   (four) weeks after the Purchase Price has been paid and the Vessel has been delivered.   193

f) Any such additional documents as may reasonably be required by the competent authorities   194
   for the purpose of registering the Vessel, provided the Buyers notify the Sellers of any such 195
   documents as soon as possible after the date of this Agreement.   196

At the time of delivery the Buyers and Sellers shall sign and deliver to each other a Protocol of 197
Delivery and Acceptance confirming the date and time of delivery of the Vessel from the Sellers
to the   198
Buyers.   199

At the time of delivery the Sellers shall hand to the Buyers the classification certificate(s) as well as all   200
plans etc., which are on board the Vessel. Other certificates which are on board the Vessel shall also   201
be handed over to the Buyers unless the Sellers are required to retain same, in which case the   202
Buyers to have the right to take copies. Other technical documentation which may   203
be in the Sellers' possession shall be promptly forwarded to the Buyers at their expense, if they so   204
request. The Sellers may keep the Vessel's log books but the Buyers to have the right to take   205
copies of same.   206

1. Completion: The position under previous Saleforms

A criticism often levelled against previous editions of the Saleform was that they failed to cover completion of the sale and purchase transaction in a satisfactory manner. It was frequently necessary for the parties to negotiate an additional clause fixing the location of the closing meetings and describing (and allocating responsibility for the preparation and procurement of) the documents to be delivered at the closing meeting ashore. If this was not done, it often gave rise to disputes during the lead up to completion. While the documents required for any given sale may differ slightly, there are several standard documents which will almost always be needed, and clause 8 of the 1993 form seeks to address this point. The new clause 8 provision can be divided into four parts.

2. Completion: The position under Saleform 1993

(1) Closing meeting ashore

First, the parties are invited to agree (and insert at line 176 of the memorandum) the place where the closing meeting ashore is to be held: see paragraph 3 on pages 124–127 of the main text.

(2) Delivery protocol

(a) Second, clause 8 (lines 197–199) requires the parties to sign a protocol of delivery and acceptance recording the date and time of the ship's delivery. This reflects market practice: see paragraph 8 on pages 122–123 in the main text.

(b) Sellers sometimes try to put words into the protocol saying that the ship has been delivered in the condition required by the contract and that sellers have performed all of their obligations under the contract.

(c) Buyers would be well advised to reject such words for they are designed to prevent buyers from raising claims against sellers in respect of defects which come to light after delivery. In the usual case, buyers will not have an opportunity to make a thorough inspection of the ship at the time of delivery and they should not be prevented by the wording of the protocol from bringing genuine claims in respect of contractual defects which are discovered after delivery; the protocol is supposed to be a timing document only and should be neutral about liability.

(d) The question of whether buyers have a right to reject the ship after signing a delivery protocol and accepting the ship (and the circumstances in which any such right could be lost) are discussed in paragraph 5 on pages 44–47 below.

(3) Documents for delivery at completion

Thirdly, clause 8 identifies the documents to be delivered by sellers at the closing meeting ashore. Broadly speaking, buyers will wish to receive documents which (as far as any documents can) confirm the ship's legal condition (i.e., her registration, sellers' title, and the registration of any security interests and other encumbrances on the ship), as well as her classification and trading status. Paragraphs a) to e) of clause 8 therefore make provision for the production of:

(a) a notarially attested and legalised bill of sale[9] (usually buyers will require sellers to deliver a specified minimum number of originals and copies);

(b) a certificate of ownership (usually buyers will wish to provide that this certificate is to be issued by the competent authorities of sellers' flag state as close as possible to completion and not earlier than a specified number of days before completion);

(c) a confirmation of class (this certificate will show the ship's "paper" classification status, as given in her class records, and will reveal whether those records contain any recommendations or conditions of class—usually buyers will wish to ensure that this certificate is issued by the ship's classification society as close as possible to completion and not earlier than a specified number of days before completion: see paragraph 5(2)(c) on page 178 of the main text);

(d) a certificate of freedom from registered encumbrances (it will not be possible for sellers to obtain this certificate before completion if the ship is subject to a registered mortgage—but buyers may require sellers to procure the issue of a certificate showing the registered encumbrances to be deleted on completion and stipulate that

___

9. The new British form is set out in Appendix 7 on pages 103–104 below.

this certificate is to be issued as close as possible to completion and not earlier than a specified number of days before completion); and

(e) a certificate of deletion from the ship's registry or a deletion undertaking—see paragraph (10) on page 123 of the main text—this requirement will not apply, and should be struck out, if buyers intend to register the ship under sellers' flag.

(4) Documents to be delivered on board

(a) Fourthly, clause 8 requires sellers to hand over the classification and other certificates/plans on board the ship at the moment when the ship is delivered to buyers. However, where sellers are required (e.g., by flag state rules) to retain (and return to the authorities of their flag state) any of the ship's original certificates, buyers' right under clause 8 will be to have copies of the relevant certificates retained by sellers.

(b) Buyers also have the right to have copies of the ship's log books and, if they pay for the forwarding costs, any other technical documents which were not kept on-board and handed over at delivery.

(5) Registration of the ship

(a) Buyers will also wish to ensure that sellers deliver all of the documents needed to enable buyers to register the ship permanently under their chosen flag. There are two points which buyers must watch for here:

> (i) by the time when the contract is made buyers may not have decided whether, or where, to reflag the ship; and
>
> (ii) even if buyers have decided these points by that time, the documentary requirements laid down by the registration authorities of buyers' chosen flag may change in the period between the conclusion of the contract and the delivery of the ship.

(b) Clause 8f) covers both of these points by requiring sellers to provide buyers with such additional documents as may reasonably be required by the authorities of buyers' chosen flag, provided that buyers notify their requirements in this respect as soon as possible after the date of the contract. This change reflects market practice: see paragraph 5(2)(p) on page 178 of the main text.

3. Sellers' authorities

(1) Limited proof

Although clause 8a) of the 1993 form requires sellers to deliver a notarised and legalised bill of sale at completion, the clause does not require sellers to produce any other proof of their authority to make and perform the sale contract.

(2) Buyers' and lenders' requirements

Buyers (and, where their acquisition of the ship is being financed by an external loan, their lenders) may wish to be satisfied that sellers' execution and performance of the contract has been duly authorised.

(3) Sellers' authority

Depending upon sellers' constitution and the identity of the person or persons signing (and otherwise handling the sale) on their behalf, sellers' authority to execute and perform the contract may be evidenced by a certificate of good standing, a board resolution, a shareholders' resolution and a power of attorney or a combination of such documents.

(4) Flag state authority

In addition, the laws of the ship's existing flag state may require sellers to obtain a written sale permission without which it may be impossible to de-register sellers' title or register the ship in buyers' name under the ship's pre-delivery flag or under a different flag.

(5) Buyers' note

If buyers wish to cover these internal and external authority issues, they may do so by negotiating for an appropriate amendment to the printed terms of clause 8: see sub-paragraphs 5(2)(a)–(e) and (j) on pages 177–178 of the main text.

4. *Nipponsale 1993*

Clause 3 of the Japanese form:
   (a) invites the parties to agree (and insert into the contract) the place where the completion meeting ashore is to be held; and
   (b) requires sellers to deliver to buyers at completion:
     (i) a notarised bill of sale;
     (ii) a deletion undertaking; and
     (iii) such other documents as may be mutually agreed—in order to minimise the risk of disputes arising in the run up to delivery, the parties would be well advised to agree these "*other documents*", and insert a concise description of them into the memorandum, before the Nipponsale contract is concluded.

CLAUSE 9—ENCUMBRANCES

9. Encumbrances   207

The Sellers warrant that the Vessel, at the time of delivery, is free from all charters, encumbrances,   208
mortgages and maritime liens or any other debts whatsoever. The Sellers hereby undertake   209
to indemnify the Buyers against all consequences of claims made against the Vessel which have   210
been incurred prior to the time of delivery.   211

1. *Mortgages*

(1) Saleform 1987

In clause 9 of the 1987 form, sellers warrant that, on delivery, the ship will be free from "*all encumbrances and maritime liens or any other debts whatsoever*".

(2) Saleform 1993

In line 209 of the 1993 form, the wording of sellers' warranty has been extended by the inclusion of a reference to *"mortgages"*. Under English law, a ship mortgage would be covered by *"encumbrances"* in clause 9 of the 1987 form[10] but it is obviously sensible to clarify this point in case the parties chose to make the memorandum subject to another system at law.

2. *Charters*

(1) New reference

The Saleform 1993 warranty has also been extended by the insertion of a reference to *"charters"*; this insertion reflects market practice—see paragraph 3 on pages 172–174 of the main text.

(2) Buyers' note

Buyers may wish to widen the scope of this reference to make it clear that the ship is to be delivered free of all trading commitments, whether they arise under bills of lading, affreightment contracts, pooling agreements, charterparties or any other commercial arrangements.

3. *Port state control*

(1) Three port state control agreements

(a) There are presently three co-operative regional port state control agreements. These are the Paris Memorandum of Understanding, the Viña del Mar Agreement and the Tokyo Memorandum of Understanding. The main participants in these agreements are listed in Appendix 8 at page 107 below.

(b) In addition, the US coastguard operates its own inspection and enforcement system and plans are in hand to establish a port state control regime in the Caribbean.

(2) Purpose of port state control

The purpose of the port state control initiative is to eliminate substandard shipping by ensuring that merchant ships visiting the ports of participating countries comply with internationally agreed standards of design, maintenance and operation.

(3) Port state control detentions

Deficiencies found by port state control inspectors have to be remedied and where inspectors decide that a ship poses a danger to safety, health or the environment they may detain or delay departure of the ship until the deficiency has been remedied.

---

10. See the decision of the Court of Appeal in *The Barenbels* [1985] 1 Lloyd's Rep. 528, and paragraph 2 on pages 128 and 129 of the main text.

(4) Port state control detentions and clause 9 of Saleform 1993

It is not clear whether buyers would be protected by clause 9 of the 1993 form in circumstances where they are deprived of the use of the ship on or soon after delivering by a port state control detention which is referable to the ship's condition on delivery under the contract; such a detention may not amount to a "*claim*" against the ship within the meaning of clause 9. In view of the increasing vigilance of port state control inspectors,[11] buyers sometimes seek to cover this point by negotiating for an appropriate amendment to the printed terms of clause 9.

4. Nature of sellers' clause 9 obligations

(1) The warranty

(a) Where buyers have good grounds for believing that, on delivery, the ship will not be in the condition warranted by sellers in lines 208 and 209 of the 1993 form, buyers' contractual rights will depend on whether the promise made by sellers in those lines is, in legal terms, a warranty, a condition or an innominate (or intermediate) term: see paragraph 4 on pages 71–75 of the main text.

(b) If sellers' promise is a warranty, buyers may claim for any loss which they suffer in consequence of sellers' breach of the warranty. However, buyers will not be entitled to refuse to take delivery of the ship.

(c) If sellers' promise is a condition, buyers may refuse to take delivery of the ship.

(d) If sellers' promise is an innominate (or intermediate) term, buyers' contractual rights will depend on how serious sellers' breach turns out to be; if the breach and/or its consequences are serious, buyers may refuse to take delivery of the ship.

(e) It will be seen from paragraphs (a) to (d) above that the effect of non-performance of the promise made by sellers in lines 208 and 209 will depend on how that promise is categorised and, if the promise is categorised as an innominate (or intermediate) term, on the nature and/or consequences of sellers' breach of contract.

(f) In practice, buyers sometimes move to avoid any uncertainty in this regard by negotiating for an amendment to the first sentence of clause 9 which strengthens their legal hand by expressly converting the "*warranty*" into a contractual "*condition*", any breach of which by sellers will entitle buyers to refuse to accept delivery of the ship.

(2) The indemnity

(a) The indemnity language (in lines 209–211 of Saleform 1993) has been reworked but not changed in substance.

(b) On a first reading of the indemnity language, buyers may be drawn to the conclusion that sellers must deal directly with any claims made against the ship for

11. Under the Paris MOU participating countries aim to inspect one in every four ships calling at their ports: in 1985 they inspected 7,879 ships and detained or delayed 356 ships; in 1993 11,252 ships were inspected and 1,105 ships were detained or delayed.

which they are responsible under clause 9. For example, where a claimant arrests the ship after delivery in respect of a claim which arose before delivery, buyers may believe that they can require sellers to:

> (i) obtain the ship's release by securing or paying off the claim; and/or
> (ii) take over the defence of the claim.

(c) However, in practice, the words used in lines 209–211 oblige buyers to:

> (i) contest the claimant's action against the ship and obtain the ship's release from arrest; and
> (ii) seek an indemnity from sellers (see paragraph 4 on page 130 of the main text).

(d) This could put buyers at a serious disadvantage, particularly if the evidence needed to defend a claim is in the possession or under the control of sellers. In such circumstances it is not clear whether the courts would be prepared to imply a term into the sale contract requiring sellers to assist buyers with the defence of the claim. Accordingly, where their bargaining position permits them to do so, it may be better for buyers to remove this uncertainty by an appropriate amendment to the printed terms of clause 9.

CLAUSE 10—TAXES, ETC.

10. Taxes, etc.   212

Any taxes, fees and expenses in connection with the purchase and registration under the Buyers' flag   213
shall be for the Buyers' account, whereas similar charges in connection with the closing of the Sellers' 214
register shall be for the Sellers' account.   215

1. Buyers' note

The printed terms of this clause have not been amended but, in practice, buyers sometimes seek to give the clause balance by inserting the words "*the sale and*" after "*with*" in line 214.

CLAUSE 11—CONDITION ON DELIVERY

11. Condition on delivery   216

The Vessel with everything belonging to her shall be at the Sellers' risk and expense until she is   217
delivered to the Buyers, but subject to the terms and conditions of this Agreement she shall be   218
delivered and taken over as she was at the time of inspection, fair wear and tear excepted.   219
However, the Vessel shall be delivered with her class maintained without condition/recommendation*,   220
free of average damage affecting the Vessel's class, and with her classification certificates and   221
national certificates, as well as all other certificates the Vessel had at the time of inspection, valid and 222
unextended without condition/recommendation* by Class or the relevant authorities at the time of   223
delivery.   224

"Inspection" in this Clause 11, shall mean the Buyers' inspection according to Clause 4a) or 4b), if   225
applicable, or the Buyers' inspection prior to the signing of this Agreement. If the Vessel is taken
over without inspection,   226

1. Saleform 1987 position

(1) Clause 11

One of the most controversial areas of dispute under the 1987 form relates to the ship's condition on delivery, and the notification of items of damage to the ship's classification society. Clause 11 of the 1987 form sets out the broad proposition that the ship is to be delivered "*as she is at the time of inspection, fair wear and tear excepted*". The clause then continues:

"*However, the vessel shall be delivered with present class free of recommendations. Sellers shall notify the Classification Society of any matters coming to their knowledge prior to delivery which upon being reported to the Classification Society would lead to the withdrawal of the vessel's class or to the imposition of a recommendation relating to her class.*"

(2) Clause 11 disputes

This provision has often given rise to disputes:

(a) as to what conditions affected (or would affect) class, and
(b) from what date matters coming to sellers' notice have to be reported,

and these difficulties are compounded where (as they frequently do) the parties incorporate additional typed words such as "*free of average damage*" without adequately explaining the relationship between the printed and typed obligations; see paragraph 3 on pages 133–138, and paragraph 3 on page 172, of the main text.

2. Saleform 1993 revision

(1) New exceptions to "as is" rule

(a) With these points in mind, the provisions of clause 11 have been significantly revised in Saleform 1993.

(b) First, although the basic obligation to deliver the ship "*as she is at the time of inspection*" is maintained, the exceptions to this rule are substantially changed. Under Saleform 1993 sellers must deliver the ship:

(i) with her class maintained free of any class conditions or recommendations;
(ii) free of average damage affecting the ship's class (average damage was defined in *The Alfred Trigon* (1981)[12] to mean damage ordinarily covered by insurance as opposed to defects resulting from wear and tear or general old age); and
(iii) with the ship's class/national/other certificates valid and unextended and free from any conditions or recommendations—see paragraph (8) on pages 134 and 135 of the main text.

12. [1981] 2 Lloyd's Rep. 333.

(c) Secondly, the Saleform 1987 provision requiring sellers to notify the ship's classification society of matters coming to their knowledge prior to delivery which could affect class has been omitted entirely.

(d) Thirdly, clause 11 of Saleform 1993 makes it clear (in lines 225 to 227) that the *"inspection"* references in lines 219 and 222 are to:

(i) buyers' pre-contract inspection of the ship under clause 4 a); or

(ii) if the 4a) alternative does not apply (see paragraphs 1 and 2 on page 9 above), buyers post-contract inspection of the ship under clause 4 b); or

(iii) if buyers have not inspected the ship under clauses 4 a) and 4 b), the date of the contract.

3. Significance of Saleform 1993 revision

(1) Buyers' position improved

(a) To a certain extent the changes noted above offset each other. On the one hand, buyers' position is improved because the reference to average damage (see paragraph 2(1)(b)(ii) above) introduces a physical element into clause 11; the ship is required not only to have an unblemished class rating on paper, she must also be physically free of any average damage affecting class at the time when sellers give NOR (see the commentary on clauses 3 and 5a) at pages 7 and 14 above) and at the moment when she is delivered to buyers.

(b) The introduction of the *"free of average damage"* requirement reflects market practice to a certain extent: see paragraph (8) on pages 134 and 135 of the main text. However, there may be circumstances in which sellers will negotiate for the deletion of the average damage requirement.

(2) Buyers' position weakened

(a) On the other hand, buyers' position is weakened by the deletion of the notification requirement (see paragraph 2(3) above) because, although this change does not derogate from any duty on sellers' part to report new matters to the ship's classification society (a duty which may arise out of the relationship between sellers and the classification society itself) it does relieve sellers of such a duty in the context of their contractual relationship with buyers.

(b) It may also be noted that sellers' duty under clause 11 of the 1987 form is to notify class of *"any matters"* which would lead to the withdrawal of class or a class recommedation, and such *"matters"* might include damage which is not *"average damage"*. So buyers may conclude that the removal of sellers' notification duty and the inclusion of the average damage requirement does not amount to an evenly balanced trade-off.

4. Buyers' reaction to clause 11 of Saleform 1993

(1) Buyers' choice

Under English law, the duty to report new class matters will not be implied into the sale contract: see *The Buena Trader* (1978),[13] discussed at paragraph 3(2) on pages 132–133 of the main text. If buyers are not prepared to accept the omission of the reporting duty, then either:

(i) they could try to persuade sellers to base the contract on Saleform 1987; or

(ii) alternatively, they could try to reinstate the Saleform 1987 notification requirement by a negotiated amendment to the printed terms of clause 11 of Saleform 1993.

(1) Buyers' note

However, in view of the difficulties to which the notification requirement has given rise (of the two main recent cases on clause 11 of the 1987 form, *The World Horizon* [14] went to the Court of Appeal and *The Niobe*[15, 16 & 17] went to the House of Lords), buyers would do well to insist on a tightly worded amendment.

5. The Niobe: *Application where class reporting requirement still applies*

(1) Decision of the Commercial Court[15]

(a) In *The "Niobe"* (1993) the Commercial Court was asked to decide whether, on a true construction of clause 11 in Saleform 1983, sellers were under an obligation to notify the ship's classification society prior to delivery of matters which affected the ship's class and which came to their knowledge:

(i) as from the date of the sale contract; or

(ii) as from the date of the last class survey of the equipment in question before the date of the sale contract; or

(iii) as from some other and, if so what, date?

(b) The Commercial Court held that the period before delivery during which sellers were obliged to notify the classification society of new matters coming to their knowledge started with the completion of the society's last survey of the relevant equipment before the date of the sale contract.

(2) Decision of the Court of Appeal [16]

Sellers appealed to the Court of Appeal which allowed their appeal holding that the period before delivery during which sellers were obliged to notify the classification society of new matters coming to their knowledge started with the date of the sale contract.

13. [1978] 2 Lloyd's Rep. 325.
14. [1993] 2 Lloyd's Rep. 56, and see also pp. 135–136 in the main text.
15. [1993] 2 Lloyd's Rep. 52, and see also pp. 136–138 in the main text.
16. [1994] 1 Lloyd's Rep. 487.

(3) Decision of the House of Lords[17]

(a) Buyers appealed to the House of Lords and argued:

(i) the class reporting requirement was put into clause 11 of Saleform 1983 to plug the gap exposed in *The Buena Trader*[13] by making sellers' reporting obligation under Saleform co-extensive with sellers' reporting obligation under the rules of their classification society;

(ii) in this case, sellers' obligation under the applicable class rules was to inform the classification society of matters affecting the ship's class whenever such matters came to their knowledge; and

(iii) it followed that sellers' obligation under clause 11 of the sale contract was to notify their classification society before delivery of all matters affecting class, whether such matters came to sellers' knowledge before or after the date of the sale contract.

(b) Sellers argued that they were obliged to notify their classification society of any matters coming to their knowledge after the date of the contract, but not before, even if such notification would inevitably have resulted in the withdrawal of the ship's class.

(c) The Lords preferred buyers' arguments and, in the course of the leading judgment, Lord McKay LC observed that while buyers' construction of clause 11 produced a commercially sensible result, sellers' interpretation of the clause could produce startling consequences. For example, sellers' interpretation could lead to a situation in which sellers would be allowed to conceal defects coming to their knowledge over what might be a lengthy period of 4 or 5 years between completion of the ship's last special survey by class and the making of the sale contract, but then would be obliged to reveal defects coming to their knowledge in the much shorter period between the making of the contract and the delivery of the ship to buyers.

(d) In the result, the House of Lords allowed buyers' appeal and held that sellers were under an obligation to notify the classification society before delivery of all matters which affected class and which came to their knowledge before or after the date of the sale contract. However, the Lords recognised that sellers need not inform the classification society of what the society already knew. So, in practice, it will not usually be necessary to go back beyond the date of the last classification survey of the relevant equipment.

(e) The decision of the House of Lords in *The Niobe* will be relevant where:

(i) the parties base the sale contract on Saleform 1987; or

(ii) the parties deal on the basis of Saleform 1993 but buyers reinstate the reporting requirement by a negotiated amendment to the printed terms of the 1993 form.

17. House of Lords transcript dated 23 March 1995.

6. Class recommendations

(1) Relevance of class rules and ship's condition

The question of whether or not a ship is subject to any class recommendations on delivery will depend on the particular rules of the ship's classification society as well as on the ship's physical condition at that time.

(2) When and how do class recommendations arise?

(a) If a class surveyor decides, before delivery, that a recommendation should be imposed, does the surveyor's decision take effect as soon as it is communicated to sellers or does a recommendation only arise after the surveyor has communicated his decision to, and had it confirmed by, the society's head office?

(b) These questions arose in *The "Andreas P"* (1994),[18] where buyers carried out steel renewal works on the ship after delivery and claimed that the cost of those works should be borne by sellers, arguing that the works were done to comply with recommendations issued by a surveyor of the ship's classification society before the ship was delivered to buyers. Sellers denied liability, saying that no recommendations were made prior to delivery.

(c) On the particular facts of the case, the judge decided that buyers' conduct precluded them from claiming the costs of the renewal works. However, it is clear from the judgment that:

(i) where a classification society surveyor requires a specified course of action to be taken as a condition of a ship remaining in class, the surveyor's requirement could constitute a recommendation;

(ii) where damage is suspected or known (but the nature and extent of the damage, and the repairs needed to make it good, can only be ascertained after a considerable delay) and the surveyor requires an inspection to be carried out and repairs to be made if found necessary, it may not be possible for sellers to describe the ship as having her class maintained free of recommendation; and

(iii) damage to a ship may be such as to affect her clean certificate of class even if the damage does not eventually lead to any formal recommendation being imposed by the ship's classification society.

7. Buyers' note

Although lines 221 to 224 in clause 11 of the 1993 form provide that the ship's certificates are to be valid and unextended without any recommendations at the time of delivery, buyers sometimes negotiate for an amendment to the effect that the ship's class and trading certificates must be clean and valid on delivery and for an agreed period (e.g., six months) from delivery.

---

18. [1994] 2 Lloyd's Rep. 183.

8. *Nipponsale 1993*

(1) **Delivery condition**

Clause 5 of the Japanese form requires sellers to deliver the ship to buyers in substantially the same condition as when the ship was inspected by buyers, fair wear
and tear excepted, but free from outstanding recommendations and average damage
affecting her present class and with all her class, national and international trading
certificates clean and valid at delivery.

(2) **Risk**

Clause 9 of the Japanese form provides that the ship (and everything belonging to
her) shall be at sellers' risk and expense until she is delivered to buyers, and after the
ship has been delivered "*in accordance with this Agreement*" sellers shall have no
responsibility for any possible fault or deficiency of any description.

CLAUSE 12—NAME/MARKINGS

12. Name/markings   230

Upon delivery the Buyers undertake to change the name of the Vessel and alter funnel markings.   231

1. *No amendments*

This clause has not been amended.

CLAUSE 13—BUYERS' DEFAULT

13. Buyers' default   232

Should the deposit not be paid in accordance with Clause 2, the Sellers have the right to cancel this   233
Agreement, and they shall be entitled to claim compensation for their losses and for all expenses   234
incurred together with interest.   235
Should the Purchase Price not be paid in accordance with Clause 3, the Sellers have the right to   236
cancel the Agreement, in which case the deposit together with interest earned shall be released to the   237
Sellers. If the deposit does not cover their loss, the Sellers shall be entitled to claim further   238
compensation for their losses and for all expenses incurred together with interest.   239

1. *Removal of interest rate fix*

Although various drafting changes have been made to the terms of this clause, the
only substantial change is that the fixed rate of interest (12 per cent per annum) provided for in clause 13 of the 1987 form has been omitted from clause 13 in Saleform
1993. This change reflects market practice—see paragraph 8 on page 144 of the
main text.

2. *Nipponsale 1993*

(1) **Sellers' right to receive liquidated damages**

Clause 7 of the Japanese form provides that:

   (a) if buyers fail to take over the ship within three banking days from their receipt
of sellers' NOR they are obliged to pay sellers, as liquidated damages for the delay,

an agreed sum per day (the daily rate for which is to be agreed and inserted in line 89 of the Japanese form); and

(b) the liquidated damages period "*shall not exceed 10 days*".

(2) Sellers' right to cancel

Clause 10 of the Japanese form provides that:

(a) if buyers fail to fulfil the contract, sellers may cancel the contract and forfeit the deposit; and

(b) if the deposit does not cover the loss suffered by sellers as a result of buyers' non-fulfilment of the contract, sellers may claim further compensation from buyers.

CLAUSE 14—SELLERS' DEFAULT

14. Sellers' default 240

Should the Sellers fail to give Notice of Readiness in accordance with Clause 5a) or fail to be ready   241
to validly complete a legal transfer by the date stipulated in line 61 the Buyers shall have   242
the option of cancelling this Agreement provided always that the Sellers shall be granted a   243
maximum of 3 banking days after Notice of Readiness has been given to make arrangements   244
for the documentation set out in Clause 8. If after Notice of Readiness has been given but before   245
the Buyers have taken delivery, the Vessel ceases to be physically ready for delivery and is not   246
made physically ready again in every respect by the date stipulated in line 61 and new Notice of   247
Readiness given, the Buyers shall retain their option to cancel. In the event that the buyers elect   248
to cancel this Agreement the deposit together with interest earned shall be released to them   249
immediately.   250

Should the Sellers fail to give Notice of Readiness by the date stipulated in line 61 or fail to be ready   251
to validly complete a legal transfer as aforesaid they shall make due compensation to the Buyers for   252
their loss and for all expenses together with interest if their failure is due to proven   253
negligence and whether or not the Buyers cancel this Agreement.   254

1. New definition of sellers' default

The opening part of the new clause 14 provides that if sellers fail to give NOR in accordance with clause 5a), or fail to be ready to validly complete a legal transfer by the contractual cancelling date, buyers may cancel the contract provided always that sellers shall have a maximum of three banking days after NOR has been given to make arrangements for the documentation set out in clause 8. Clause 14 then goes on to state that if, after sellers have given a valid NOR, the ship "*ceases*" to be physically ready for delivery and is not made physically ready again (and a fresh NOR given) within the contractual cancelling date, buyers retain their option to cancel.

2. Significance of new provisions

(1) Failure to give NOR

The new provisions call for a number of comments. First, the new clause 14 provides that buyers may cancel the sale contract "*if sellers fail to give NOR in accordance with clause 5a)*". This could be taken to mean that, where sellers' NOR is invalid (through non-compliance with either or both of the ship location and physical readiness requirements), buyers may cancel the sale contract irrespective of whether there would be enough time for sellers to put matters right and issue a fresh NOR before the contractual cancelling date. This, however, must be doubtful. Sellers would no doubt argue that, if they still have time to serve a new NOR, they have not yet "*failed*" to do so.

(2) Sellers' duty to give NOR

Secondly, and conversely, line 56 in clause 5a) provides that once the ship is at the place of delivery and physically ready for delivery, sellers "*shall*" give NOR. This could be taken to mean that if sellers are in a position to give notice but fail to do so (in circumstances when there are still several days left before the cancelling date), buyers may be entitled to cancel on the basis that sellers have failed to give NOR in accordance with clause 5a).

(3) NOR given before cancelling date but delivery made after cancelling date

(a) Thirdly, there is some lack of clarity as to whether buyers may cancel if delivery of the ship occurs after the cancelling date, but the NOR is served on or before it. A failure to "*be ready to validly complete a legal transfer*" by the cancelling date is expressed to give buyers the option to cancel. But, as stated above, clause 3 requires buyers to pay the purchase price within three banking days of their receipt of a valid NOR and clause 14 allows sellers up to three banking days from service of a valid NOR within which to make ready the clause 8 delivery documents.

(b) There is, therefore, tension between these provisions. Their combined effect appears to mean that the Saleform 1993 cancelling date is not a drop dead date for all purposes, but merely the last date upon which sellers may give NOR. If that is right, it means that, if the ship is in all respects physically ready for delivery at the place of delivery and sellers give NOR on the cancelling date, they will have up to 3 banking days after the NOR has been given (and after the cancelling date has passed) within which to deliver the ship and the clause 8 delivery documents. Apparently, this is what the promoters of the 1993 form intended, and most commentators appear to take the view that this is what they have achieved. Indeed, the words "*provided always*" in the passage referred to above support this conclusion; but clause 14 of Saleform 1993 is not as clear as it might be on the point.

(4) Buyers' note

In practice, some buyers may seek to provide (by brief amendments to the printed terms of clauses 3, 5a) and 14 of the Saleform 1993) that sellers cannot give a valid NOR until the ship and her dosuments are in all respects physically and legally ready at the place of delivery; ready, that is, except in relation to specified aspects of delivery (such as sellers' removal of items excluded from the sale or the release and deletion of any mortgages over the ship) which are to be accomplished immediately before, or upon, delivery: see paragraph 3(3) at page 8 above.

3. *Buyers' right to claim "compensation"*

(1) Sellers' default

(a) The concluding part of clause 14 in the 1993 form (in lines 251–254) provides that if sellers fail to give NOR by the cancelling date specified in line 61, or fail to be ready to validly complete the legal transfer of the ship within 3 banking days after NOR has been given, and (in either case) their default is due to proven negligence, they must compensate buyers for their *"loss and for all expenses together with interest"* irrespective of whether buyers cancel the contract. The reference to *"all expenses"* does not appear in clause 14 of the 1987 form and its inclusion in the 1993 form therefore enlarges the express contractual *"compensation"* which buyers may claim.

(b) The first point to note about the *"proven negligence"* requirement is that it is expressed to apply only to the two types of default described in lines 251 and 252; it is not expressed to apply to other types of default such as non-compliance with the ship's description (see paragraph 2(2) on pages 4–5 above) or breach of clause 11. This means that where sellers' breach of contract is not a default of the type described in lines 251 and 252, the *"proven negligence"* requirement will not apply and buyers will be entitled to exercise the remedies available to them under the general law.

(c) The second point to note about the *"proven negligence"* requirement is that the precise relationship between buyers' right to *"compensation"* under lines 251 to 254 and buyers' right to claim damages under the general law for sellers' breach of contract is not really spelt out.

(d) Buyers' right to cancel is not dependent on breach. If there is no independent breach, buyers' right to *"compensation"* will depend on buyers being able to comply with the requirements set out in lines 251 to 254, and no independent right to damages will arise.

(e) It is possible, however, to envisage a situation where a failure to give NOR or to complete a legal transfer may also give rise to independent breaches of contract, for example: a failure to give NOR when the ship is ready contrary to clause 5a); or a refusal to give NOR showing an intention on sellers' part not to be bound by the sale contract. In those examples, if buyers cannot show that sellers' failure (or refusal) to give NOR was due to proven negligence, would buyers nevertheless be entitled to claim general damages for sellers' breach of contract, rather than *"compensation"* for negligence? Or would clause 14 operate so as to exclude buyers' right to claim general damages in such circumstances?

(f) As a matter of principle (and subject to the rare occasions on which the Unfair Contract Terms Act 1977 will apply to commercial ship sale contacts—see paragraph 1(2) on page 63 of the main text), exclusion provisions are generally effective under English law but (because they are designed to take away fundamental rights which could otherwise be available to a party) they will be interpreted strictly by judges and arbitrators. This means that if there is room for argument as to the meaning or scope of such a provision, the benefit of the doubt will not be given to the party seeking to rely on the exclusion. Clause 14 of the 1993 form is not as clear as it might be in relation to the question of whether buyers may sue sellers in contract where they cannot prove negligence in relation to, say, a failure to give NOR by the cancelling date; but the uncertainty could be resolved by an appropriate amendment to the printed terms of clause 14.

(2) Invalid NOR remedied but buyers suffer loss

(a) The position under clause 14 of the 1993 form is also unclear where:

(i) buyers incur costs (e.g., the board, lodging and salary expenses for their take-over crew and loan drawdown costs) in reliance on sellers' NOR;

(ii) the NOR proves to be invalid (the invalidity being due to proven negligence);

(iii) buyers do not cancel the contract; and

(iv) sellers subsequently put matters right and issue a fresh NOR before expiry of the contractual cancelling date.

(b) Curiously, in such circumstances, clause 14 of the 1993 form does not expressly oblige sellers to compensate buyers for any additional (i.e., wasted) costs which they incur in reliance on the invalid NOR. However, buyers may be entitled to recover such losses, if they are reasonably foreseeable, under general principles of English law; and, of course, buyers may seek to put the issue beyond doubt by negotiating for an appropriate amendment to the printed terms of clause 14.

4. Causes of sellers' default

(1) Proven negligence

As noted in paragraph 3(1)(a) above, clause 14 of Saleform 1993 provides that buyers' right to claim *"compensation"* for certain of sellers' defaults (as opposed to general damages for breach of contract—see paragraphs 3(1)(c)–(f) above) will depend on whether the default in question is due to *"proven negligence"*. In contrast, clause 14 in the 1987 form refers expressly to the *"proven negligence of ... [sellers]"*. The explanatory notes issued by BIMCO in relation to Saleform 1993 do not refer to this change of wording and so it is not clear what significance (if any) is to be attached to this change of emphasis.

(2) Causes of maritime accidents: High percentage due to human error

(a) Recently, the authors of *Safer Ships, Cleaner Seas*[19] wrote:

Most experts agree that human error accounts for between 60% and 80% of all accidents. The UK P&I Club's analysis of major claims between 1987 and 1992 supports this, with 63% of major claims directly attributable to human error.[20] As a comparison, 28% of major claims were caused by structural, mechanical or equipment failure, which indicates that whilst operational error is the major direct cause "hardware" failure can also be a significant problem. Of course most accidents are caused by a combination of "hardware" and "software" factors and most equipment or structural failures will ultimately have resulted from human failure, perhaps through carelessness in design, construction or maintenance at an earlier stage.

19. The report of Lord Donaldson's inquiry into the prevention of pollution from merchant shipping (1994, HMSO, ISBN 0-10 125 602-7).

20. The United Kingdom Mutual Steam Ship Assurance Association (Bermuda) Limited–*Analysis of Major Claims 1993*.

(b) Where sellers' default is referable to human error which may be categorised as "*negligent*", difficult questions may arise as to whether sellers are responsible for all negligent acts on their side of their contractual divide. Some of these questions are discussed in paragraphs (3) to (5) below.

(3) Events beyond sellers' control

Where sellers' failure to comply with, say, the NOR requirements of the contract is due to external events or circumstances which are beyond their control and for which they are not in any way responsible (for example, the ship is involved in a collision for which the other ship is fully to blame) it is strongly arguable that sellers would not be liable to "*compensate*" buyers because there is no "*proven negligence*" which is in any sense attributable to sellers. However, as noted at paragraphs 3(1)(c)–(f) above, the question of whether buyers might be entitled to recover general damages if they can establish an independent breach of contract by sellers (as opposed to "*compensation*" for negligence) remains to be determined.

(4) Events within sellers' sphere of responsibility

Where sellers' default falls within the category of defaults described in lines 251 and 252 of the 1993 form and is due to proven negligence on the part of sellers' management team (bearing in mind that certain key members of sellers' on board crew may be classified as "*management*"), buyers should be entitled to claim compensation from sellers. However, the position may be less clear where the person or event causing the default is within sellers' sphere of responsibility but sellers' management is not to blame in any way: see the next following paragraph.

(5) Crew negligence

(a) In a recent unreported case arising out of a contract based on Saleform 1987 disputes arose between sellers and buyers regarding sellers' responsibility for, amongst other matters, delay in the delivery of their ship.

(b) Prior to delivery the ship was operating under a bareboat charter, and sellers argued that:

(i) their delay in delivering the ship to buyers was solely and directly attributable to the negligent (and, perhaps, fraudulent) conduct of certain members of the ship's crew, all of whom had been employed and supervised by the bareboat charterer;

(ii) sellers had exercised due care in the selection and supervision of the bareboat charterer;

(iii) in committing the actions which delayed the ship, the relevant crew members were acting outside the scope of their employment as charterers' employees and outside the scope of their actual and ostensible authority as charterers' and/or sellers' agents; and

(iv) in the circumstances, the delay in delivery was not caused by "*proven negligence*" attributable to sellers.

(c) Sellers' arguments in relation to these issues were not tested in arbitration or the courts because the dispute was settled as part of a wider compromise between the parties. However, if buyers wish to make it clear that, as between sellers and buyers, sellers are to be fully responsible for all of the acts, omissions and defaults (whether negligent, fraudulent or otherwise) of their employees, or of any contractors or agents or other representatives employed or appointed by sellers, buyers could negotiate for an appropriate amendment to the printed terms of clause 14.

5. Buyers' right to reject the ship

(1) Buyers' choice

Where sellers tender delivery of a contractually defective ship and buyers have a right to reject the ship (see paragraph 5 on pages 148–149 of the main text), buyers have a choice. They may, of course, exercise their right of rejection. Alternatively, they may accept the ship, although aware of its defective condition, and bring a post-delivery claim in damages against sellers.

(2) Buyers' right to reject: Sale of Goods Act 1979 requirements

Under the Sale of Goods Act 1979, if buyers wished to reject the ship, they had to satisfy two requirements. First, they had to exercise their right unequivocally. Secondly, they could not have already "*accepted*" the ship either expressly or by implication.

(3) Difficulties created by Sale of Goods Act 1979

(a) The provisions of the 1979 Act relating to acceptance sometimes gave rise to considerable difficulties in sale of goods cases. In particular, problems arose because of the interrelation between sections 34 and 35 of the 1979 Act. Under section 34(2), unless otherwise agreed, when sellers tendered delivery of goods to buyers, sellers were bound on request to afford buyers a reasonable opportunity of examining the goods for the purpose of ascertaining whether they were in conformity with the contract. Where goods were delivered to buyers and they had not previously examined them, they were not deemed to have accepted them until they had had such an opportunity.

(b) Buyers' right to inspect under section 34(2) of the 1979 Act may be excluded by an express, or implied, agreement to the contrary between sellers and buyers. The only rights of inspection expressly given to buyers by Saleform 1993 are the rights set out in clause 4: see paragraphs 1–3 on pages 9 and 10 above. In practice, buyers may also have opportunities to view the ship:

(i) during the classification society drydocking inspection of the ship provided for in clause 6 of the 1993 form—see pages 19 to 23 above;

(ii) during any attendance on-board the ship by buyers' representatives under clause 15 of the 1993 form—see page 48 below; and

     (iii) immediately before or, depending on the closing arrangements, immediately after the on-board completion meeting—see paragraph 1(1)(d) on page 99, and paragraph 4 on page 138, of the main text.

However, these viewing opportunities do not amount to contractual rights of inspection. Some commentators believe that the express inspection provisions in the Saleform contract operate so as to exclude the application of section 34(2) of the 1979 Act. Buyers should also note that even if section 34(2) applies, the right to inspect will only arise "*on request*" by buyers.

    (c) Where buyers have a right to request an inspection under section 34(2), it is necessary to consider the interrelation between sections 34 and 35: see the next following paragraphs.

(6) Deemed acceptance by buyers under Sale of Goods Act 1979

    (a) Under section 35(1) of the 1979 Act, buyers were deemed to have accepted the goods in three situations:

      (i) when buyers intimated to sellers that they had accepted them; or

     (ii) when the goods had been delivered to buyers and they did any act in relation to the goods which was inconsistent with the ownership of sellers (subject to buyers' right to examine the goods for conformity under section 34); or

    (iii) when after the lapse of a reasonable time buyers retained the goods without intimating to sellers that they had rejected them.

    (b) Where buyers were deemed to have accepted the goods, they were restricted to a claim for damages. What, however, was the position where buyers took one of the steps outlined in section 35 before they had had a chance to inspect under section 34?

(7) Sale and Supply of Goods Act 1994

The Sale and Supply of Goods Act 1994 (which came into force on 3 January 1995, but only for contracts made after that date) has amended the rules regarding deemed acceptance and, to assess the possible application of the amendments to ship sale transactions, it is necessary to consider each of the old rules in turn.

(8) Intimation of acceptance by buyers

    (a) The first problem with section 35(1) of the 1979 Act was that, because of the rule concerning "*intimation of acceptance*", buyers could find that they had unwittingly deprived themselves of the right to reject goods, even if they had not yet had an opportunity to examine them; for example, by signing a protocol of delivery and acceptance when the goods were delivered.

    (b) Section 2(2) of the 1994 Act deals with this problem by introducing a right to a reasonable opportunity to examine the goods before any intimation of acceptance can be effective. But buyers of ships should note that:

(i) the parties to a non-consumer (i.e., commercial) sale can contract out of this provision; and

(ii) more importantly, non-consumer buyers may also waive their right to rely on this provision and buyers' signature of a protocol of delivery and acceptance could well have that effect, unless buyers qualify their signature so as to make it clear that they are reserving their right to make an inspection under this provision.

(9) Act inconsistent with sellers' ownership: sub-sales

(a) It was reasonably clear from sections 34(2) and 35(1) of the 1979 Act that buyers were not deemed to have accepted the goods under this heading until they had had an opportunity to inspect, and that remains the position.

(b) The rule concerning *"acts inconsistent with the ownership of the seller"* did, however, give rise to different difficulties, particularly where buyers resold the goods to sub-buyers. There was authority to the effect that buyers who sub-sold goods acted in a way inconsistent with the ownership of sellers. In other words, by delivering the goods to a third party following a sub-sale, buyers were taken to have no intention of rejecting the goods.

(c) Section 2(6)(b) of the 1994 Act deals with this point by providing that buyers will not be deemed to have accepted goods merely because they have sub-sold them or disposed of them in some other way. Buyers should note, however, that:

(i) if the sub-buyers do not themselves reject, so that the goods cannot be returned to the original sellers, buyers may be unable to reject for this reason but, in such a case, they are presumably less likely to wish to reject anyway; and

(ii) sellers will not need to rely on section 2(6)(b) of the 1994 Act if buyers have already lost their right of rejection by signing a protocol of delivery and acceptance in a form which is held to have that effect.

(10) Act inconsistent with sellers' ownership: Remedial works

(a) Previously, buyers who sought to have defects in goods remedied might, by implication, have intimated their acceptance of the goods or be taken to have acted in a way inconsistent with the ownership of sellers, both of which would prevent them from rejecting the goods, which they might wish to do if the attempted remedial works failed. In such cases, buyers were often held to have lost their right to reject.

(b) Section 2(6)(a) of the 1994 Act deals with this point by providing that if buyers ask for a defect to be corrected (whether by sellers or under an arrangement made with sellers) this should not of itself deprive buyers of their right to reject. In practice, where (as recently happened in an unreported case arising out of a contract based on Saleform 1987) buyers agree to accept delivery of the ship before sellers have completed necessary remedial works, buyers would be well advised to require the reservation of their contractual rights to be expressly dealt with in an addendum to the sale contract.

(11) Lapse of reasonable time

(a) According to section 59 of the 1979 Act, what is a *"reasonable time"* is a question of fact. Several recent cases have highlighted the difficulties which could arise under this provision. According to the case law, in order for a reasonable time to have elapsed, it was not necessary to allow for sufficient time for hidden defects to be discovered. Thus, the right to reject could be lost before buyers even knew of the problem.

(b) Section 2(5) of the 1994 Act still provides that buyers are deemed to have accepted goods if, after the lapse of a reasonable time, they retain them without intimating rejection. The test is, however, slightly less restrictive than previously because the questions that are material in determining whether a reasonable time has in fact elapsed are stated to include the question of whether buyers have had a reasonable opportunity to examine the goods to ascertain whether they conform with the contract. Even this will not, however, solve the problem of latent defects which only surface weeks or months after delivery has occurred; here, buyers may still lose the right to reject before they become aware of the defects.

(c) Buyers of ships should note, however, that sellers will not need to rely on section 2(5) of the 1994 Act if buyers have already lost their right of rejection by signing a protocol of delivery and acceptance in a form which is held to have that effect.

6. Removal of interest rate fix

The fixed rate of interest (12 per cent p.a.) provided for in clause 14 of the 1987 form has been omitted from clause 14 in Saleform 1993. This change reflects market practice —see paragraph 8, and paragraph 1(1)(a), both on page 144 of the main text.

7. Nipponsale 1993

Clause 14 of the Japanese form:

(1) provides that if sellers default in the delivery of the ship with everything belonging to her in the manner and within the time specified in the contract, the deposit shall be returned to buyers immediately; and

(2) requires sellers to compensate buyers for any loss which they suffer as a result of sellers' default in delivering the ship where such default is due to sellers' *"negligent or intentional acts or omissions"*.

CLAUSE 15—BUYERS' REPRESENTATIVES

15. Buyers' representatives	255
After this Agreement has been signed by both parties and the deposit has been lodged, the Buyers	256
have the right to place two representatives on board the Vessel at their sole risk and expense upon	257
arrival at on or about	258
These representatives are on board for the purpose of familiarisation and in the capacity of	259
observers only, and they shall not interfere in any respect with the operation of the Vessel. The	260
Buyers' representatives shall sign the Sellers' letter of indemnity prior to their embarkation.	261

1. Buyers' right under clause 15

(1) New provision

This is an entirely new provision giving buyers the right, when they have paid the security deposit, to place two representatives on board the ship for the purposes of familiarisation and observation only.

(2) Buyers' note

The new provision reflects market practice (see paragraph 1 on page 171 of the main text) but, depending on the particular circumstances of the transaction (for example, the expected time lag between contract and delivery), buyers will sometimes try to negotiate up the number of representatives and the period(s) during which they may travel on board the ship.

2. Sellers' note

Line 261 provides that an indemnity letter must be signed by buyers' representatives before embarkation but, in practice, sellers may negotiate for an amendment to the printed terms of this clause which requires buyers to sign the letter as well.

3. The indemnity letter

The terms of the indemnity letter will vary from case to case but for a review of some of the matters which may be covered by such a letter, see paragraph 1 on page 171 of the main text.

CLAUSE 16—ARBITRATION

16. Arbitration	262

a)*	This Agreement shall be governed by and construed in accordance with English law and	263
	any dispute arising out of this Agreement shall be referred to arbitration in London in	264
	accordance with the Arbitration Acts 1950 and 1979 or any statutory modification or	265
	re-enactment thereof for the time being in force, one arbitrator being appointed by each	266
	party. On the receipt by one party of the nomination in writing of the other party's arbitrator,	267
	that party shall appoint their arbitrator within fourteen days, failing which the decision of the	268
	single arbitrator appointed shall apply. If two arbitrators properly appointed shall not agree	269
	they shall appoint an umpire whose decision shall be final.	270
b)*	This Agreement shall be governed by and construed in accordance with Title 9 of the	271
	United States Code and the Law of the State of New York and should any dispute arise	
	out of this Agreement, the	272
	matter in dispute shall be referred to three persons at New York, one to	273
	be appointed by each of the parties hereto, and the third by the two so chosen; their	274
	decision or that of any two of them shall be final, and for purpose of enforcing any award,	275
	Agreement may be made a rule of the Court.	276
	The proceedings shall be conducted in accordance with the rules of the Society of Maritime	277
	Arbitrators, Inc. New York.	278
c)*	Any dispute arising out of this Agreement shall be referred to arbitration at	279
	, subject to the procedures applicable there.	280
	The laws of shall govern this Agreement.	281

*	*16a), 16b) and 16c) are alternatives; delete whichever is not applicable. In the absence of*	282
	deletions, alternative 16a) to apply.	283

1. *Arbitration and governing law under Saleform 1987*

(1) Dispute resolution method and location

The 1987 form provides for *"any disputes ... [arising] ... in connection with the interpretation and fulfilment"* of the sale contract to be resolved by arbitration, but leaves the arbitration venue to be agreed by the parties. If no place is chosen, arbitration will take place in London.

(2) Tribunal and governing law

The 1987 form also provides that:

(a) the arbitration will be before a sole arbitrator unless the parties cannot agree upon his or her identity, in which case the reference will be to three arbitrators; and

(b) the contract is governed by the law of the place of arbitration.

2. *Arbitration and governing law under Saleform 1993*

(1) Three alternatives

Clause 16 of Saleform 1993 introduces three alternatives for the contract's governing law and place of arbitration (two of which should be deleted by the parties):

(a) English law, with arbitration in London before two arbitrators or, if the arbitrators fail to agree, an umpire; or

(b) US law with arbitration in New York before three arbitrators; or

(c) some other system of law and place of arbitration agreed between the parties and inserted in the contract.

(2) Automatic application of English law and London arbitration

If the parties fail to make their choice clear by deleting two of the clause 16 alternatives, the English law and London arbitration alternative will apply automatically.

(3) Reference to arbitration

The 1993 form refers to arbitration *"any dispute arising out of"* the sale contract: this formulation is slightly wider than the corresponding provision in the 1987 form.

3. *Arbitration procedures under Saleform 1993*

(1) Incorporation of LMAA Terms

Curiously, while the US alternative provides that arbitration proceedings will be conducted in accordance with the rules of the Society of Maritime Arbitrators, Inc. New York, the English alternative does not refer to the well known and widely used London Maritime Arbitrators' Association (LMAA) Terms. However, the LMAA Terms may be incorporated into Saleform 1993 by an appropriate amendment to the printed terms of clause 16.

(2) New LMAA Terms and arbitration clause

The LMAA Terms (1994), together with an arbitration clause recommended by the LMAA, are set out in Appendices 5 and 6 at pages 83–100 below.

4. Nipponsale 1993

Clause 15 of the Japanese form provides for disputes to be referred to arbitration:

(a) in Tokyo;

(b) before the Tokyo Maritime Arbitration Commission (TOMAC) of the Japan Shipping Exchange; and

(c) in accordance with the TOMAC Rules.

ADDITIONAL PROVISIONS

1. Saleform 1993

(1) Appendix

Unlike some previous editions of the form, Saleform 1993 does not include a blank page entitled "*Appendix*". However, the parties to a contract based on Saleform 1993 may agree to incorporate additional provisions, for example: provisions covering blacklisting and boycotting, confidentiality, the service of notices etc—see paragraph 4 on pages 176–177, paragraph 6 on page 179, and paragraph 11 on pages 182–183, all in the main text.

(2) Incorporating additional provisions

Where the parties choose to incorporate additional provisions they would be well advised to make sure that:

(a) those provisions do not conflict with any of the printed terms of the 1993 form;

(b) are clearly expressed to form part of the contract; and

(c) are attached to the contract and signed together with (and at the same time as) the contract.

2. Nipponsale 1993

The final (unnumbered) line in the Japanese form provides "*The additional clauses from 16 to . . . shall be deemed to be fully incorporated in this Agreement*".

SECTION TWO

APPENDICES

APPENDIX 1

SALEFORM 1993

MEMORANDUM OF AGREEMENT

Norwegian Shipbrokers' Association's Memorandum of Agreement for sale and purchase of ships. Adopted by The Baltic and International Maritime Council (BIMCO) in 1956.

Code-name

SALEFORM 1993

Revised 1966, 1983 and 1986/87.

Dated:

hereinafter called the Sellers, have agreed to sell, and   1

hereinafter called the Buyers, have agreed to buy   2

Name: 3

Classification Society/Class: 4

Built: By: 5

Flag: Place of Registration: 6

Call Sign: Grt/Nrt: 7

Register Number: 8

hereinafter called the Vessel, on the following terms and conditions: 9

Definitions   10

"Banking days" are days on which banks are open both in the country of the currency   11
stipulated for the Purchase Price in Clause 1 and in the place of closing stipulated in Clause 8.   12

"In writing" or "written" means a letter handed over from the Sellers to the Buyers or vice versa,   13
a registered letter, telex, telefax or other modern form of written communication.   14

"Classification Society" or "Class" means the Society referred to in line 4.   15

1.   Purchase Price   16

2.   Deposit   17

As security for the correct fulfilment of this Agreement the Buyers shall pay a deposit of 10 %   18
(ten per cent) of the Purchase Price within   banking days from the date of this   19
Agreement. This deposit shall be placed with   20

and held by them in a joint account for the Sellers and the Buyers, to be released in accordance   21
with joint written instructions of the Sellers and the Buyers. Interest, if any, to be credited to the   22
Buyers. Any fee charged for holding the said deposit shall be borne equally by the Sellers and the   23
Buyers.   24

3.   Payment   25

The said Purchase Price shall be paid in full free of bank charges to   26

on delivery of the Vessel, but not later than 3 banking days after the Vessel is in every respect   27
physically ready for delivery in accordance with the terms and conditions of this Agreement and   28
Notice of Readiness has been given in accordance with Clause 5.   29

4.   Inspections   30

a)*   The Buyers have inspected and accepted the Vessel's classification records. The Buyers   31
         have also inspected the Vessel at/in   on   32
         and have accepted the Vessel following this inspection and the sale is outright and definite,   33
         subject only to the terms and conditions of this Agreement.   34

b)*   The Buyers shall have the right to inspect the Vessel's classification records and declare   35
         whether same are accepted or not within   36

         The Sellers shall provide for inspection of the Vessel at/in   37

         The Buyers shall undertake the inspection without undue delay to the Vessel. Should the   38
         Buyers cause undue delay they shall compensate the Sellers for the losses thereby incurred.   39
         The Buyers shall inspect the Vessel without opening up and without cost to the Sellers.   40
         During the inspection, the Vessel's deck and engine log books shall be made available for   41
         examination by the Buyers. If the Vessel is accepted after such inspection, the sale shall   42
         become outright and definite, subject only to the terms and conditions of this Agreement,   43
         provided the Sellers receive written notice of acceptance from the Buyers within 72 hours   44
         after completion of such inspection.   45
         Should notice of acceptance of the Vessel's classification records and of the Vessel not be   46
         received by the Sellers as aforesaid, the deposit together with interest earned shall be   47
         released immediately to the Buyers, whereafter this Agreement shall be null and void.   48

*   *4 a) and 4b) are alternatives; delete whichever is not applicable. In the absence of deletions,* 49
         alternative 4a) to apply.   50

5.   Notices, time and place of delivery   51

a)   The Sellers shall keep the Buyers well informed of the Vessel's itinerary and shall   52
         provide the Buyers with   ,   , and   days notice of the estimated time of arrival at the   53
         intended place of drydocking/underwater inspection/delivery. When the Vessel is at the place   54
         of delivery and in every respect physically ready for delivery in accordance with this   55
         Agreement, the Sellers shall give the Buyers a written Notice of Readiness for delivery.   56

b)   The Vessel shall be delivered and taken over safely afloat at a safe and accessible berth or   57
         anchorage at/in   58

         in the Sellers' option.   59

         Expected time of delivery: 60

         Date of cancelling (see Clauses 5 c), 6 b) (iii) and 14):   61

c)   If the Sellers anticipate that, notwithstanding the exercise of due diligence by them, the   62
         Vessel will not be ready for delivery by the cancelling date they may notify the Buyers in   63
         writing stating the date when they anticipate that the Vessel will be ready for delivery and   64
         propose a new cancelling date. Upon receipt of such notification the Buyers shall have the   65
         option of either cancelling this Agreement in accordance with Clause 14 within 7 running   66
         days of receipt of the notice or of accepting the new date as the new cancelling date. If the   67
         Buyers have not declared their option within 7 running days of receipt of the Sellers'   68
         notification or if the Buyers accept the new date, the date proposed in the Sellers' notification   69
         shall be deemed to be the new cancelling date and shall be substituted for the cancelling   70
         date stipulated in line 61.   71

         If this Agreement is maintained with the new cancelling date all other terms and conditions   72
         hereof including those contained in Clauses 5 a) and 5 c) shall remain unaltered and in full   73
         force and effect. Cancellation or failure to cancel shall be entirely without prejudice to any   74
         claim for damages the Buyers may have under Clause 14 for the Vessel not being ready by   75
         the original cancelling date.   76

d)   Should the Vessel become an actual, constructive or compromised total loss before delivery   77
        the deposit together with interest earned shall be released immediately to the Buyers   78
        whereafter this Agreement shall be null and void.   79

6.   **Drydocking/Divers Inspection**   80

a)**   The Sellers shall place the Vessel in drydock at the port of delivery for inspection by the   81
        Classification Society of the Vessel's underwater parts below the deepest load line, the   82
        extent of the inspection being in accordance with the Classification Society's rules. If the   83
        rudder, propeller, bottom or other underwater parts below the deepest load line are found   84
        broken, damaged or defective so as to affect the Vessel's class, such defects shall be made   85
        good at the Sellers' expense to the satisfaction of the Classification Society without   86
        condition/recommendation*.   87

b)**   (i)   The Vessel is to be delivered without drydocking. However, the Buyers shall   88
        have the right at their expense to arrange for an underwater inspection by a diver approved   89
        by the Classification Society prior to the delivery of the Vessel. The Sellers shall at their 90
        cost make the Vessel available for such inspection. The extent of the inspection and the   91
        conditions under which it is performed shall be to the satisfaction of the Classification   92
        Society. If the conditions at the port of delivery are unsuitable for such inspection, the   93
        Sellers shall make the Vessel available at a suitable alternative place near to the delivery   94
        port.   95

        (ii)   If the rudder, propeller, bottom or other underwater parts below the deepest load line   96
        are found broken, damaged or defective so as to affect the Vessel's class, then unless   97
        repairs can be carried out afloat to the satisfaction of the Classification Society, the Sellers   98
        shall arrange for the Vessel to be drydocked at their expense for inspection by the   99
        Classification Society of the Vessel's underwater parts below the deepest load line, the   100
        extent of the inspection being in accordance with the Classification Society's rules. If the   101
        rudder, propeller, bottom or other underwater parts below the deepest load line are found   102
        broken, damaged or defective so as to affect the Vessel's class, such defects shall be made   103
        good by the Sellers at their expense to the satisfaction of the Classification Society   104
        without condition/recommendation*. In such event the Sellers are to pay also for the cost of   105
        the underwater inspection and the Classification Society's attendance.   106

        (iii)   If the Vessel is to be drydocked pursuant to Clause 6 b) (ii) and no suitable dry-   107
        docking facilities are available at the port of delivery, the Sellers shall take the Vessel   108
        to a port where suitable drydocking facilities are available, whether within or outside the   109
        delivery range as per Clause 5 b). Once drydocking has taken place the Sellers shall deliver   110
        the Vessel at a port within the delivery range as per Clause 5 b) which shall, for the   111
        purpose of this Clause, become the new port of delivery. In such event the cancelling date   112
        provided for in Clause 5 b) shall be extended by the additional time required for the   113
        drydocking and extra steaming, but limited to a maximum of 14 running days.   114

c)   If the Vessel is drydocked pursuant to Clause 6 a) or 6 b) above   115

        (i)   the Classification Society may require survey of the tailshaft system, the extent of 116
        the survey being to the satisfaction of the Classification surveyor. If such survey is not   117
        required by the Classification Society, the Buyers shall have the right to require the tailshaft   118
        to be drawn and surveyed by the Classification Society, the extent of the survey being in   119
        accordance with the Classification Society's rules for tailshaft survey and consistent with   120
        the current stage of the Vessel's survey cycle. The Buyers shall declare whether they   121
        require the tailshaft to be drawn and surveyed not later than by the completion of the   122
        inspection by the Classification Society. The drawing and refitting of the tailshaft shall be 123
        arranged by the Sellers. Should any parts of the tailshaft system be condemned or found   124
        defective so as to affect the Vessel's class, those parts shall be renewed or made good at   125
        the Sellers' expense to the satisfaction of the Classification Society without   126
        condition/recommendation*.   127

(ii)   the expenses relating to the survey of the tailshaft system shall be borne   128
by the Buyers unless the Classification Society requires such survey to be carried out, in   129
which case the Sellers shall pay these expenses. The Sellers shall also pay the expenses   130
if the Buyers require the survey and parts of the system are condemned or found defective   131
or broken so as to affect the Vessel's class*.   132

(iii)   the expenses in connection with putting the Vessel in and taking her out of   133
drydock, including the drydock dues and the Classification Society's fees shall be paid by   134
the Sellers if the Classification Society issues any condition/recommendation* as a result   135
of the survey or if it requires survey of the tailshaft system. In all other cases the Buyers   136
shall pay the aforesaid expenses, dues and fees.   137

(iv)   the Buyers' representative shall have the right to be present in the drydock, but   138
without interfering with the work or decisions of the Classification surveyor.   139

(v)   the Buyers shall have the right to have the underwater parts of the Vessel   140
cleaned and painted at their risk and expense without interfering with the Sellers' or the   141
Classification surveyor's work, if any, and without affecting the Vessel's timely delivery. If,   142
however, the Buyers' work in drydock is still in progress when the Sellers have   143
completed the work which the Sellers are required to do, the additional docking time   144
needed to complete the Buyers' work shall be for the Buyers' risk and expense. In the event   145
that the Buyers' work requires such additional time, the Sellers may upon completion of the   146
Sellers' work tender Notice of Readiness for delivery whilst the Vessel is still in drydock   147
and the Buyers shall be obliged to take delivery in accordance with Clause 3, whether   148
the Vessel is in drydock or not and irrespective of Clause 5 b).   149

*   Notes, if any, in the surveyor's report which are accepted by the Classification Society   150
without condition/recommendation are not to be taken into account.   151

**   *6 a) and 6 b) are alternatives; delete whichever is not applicable. In the absence of deletions,*   152
alternative 6 a) to apply.   153

7.   Spares/bunkers, etc.   154

The Sellers shall deliver the Vessel to the Buyers with everything belonging to her on board and on   155
shore. All spare parts and spare equipment including spare tail-end shaft(s) and/or spare   156
propeller(s)/propeller blade(s), if any, belonging to the Vessel at the time of inspection used or   157
unused, whether on board or not shall become the Buyers' property, but spares on order are to be   158
excluded. Forwarding charges, if any, shall be for the Buyers' account. The Sellers are not required to   159
replace spare parts including spare tail-end shaft(s) and spare propeller(s)/propeller blade(s) which   160
are taken out of spare and used as replacement prior to delivery, but the replaced items shall be the   161
property of the Buyers. The radio installation and navigational equipment shall be included in the sale   162
without extra payment if they are the property of the Sellers. Unused stores and provisions shall be   163
included in the sale and be taken over by the Buyers without extra payment.   164

The Sellers have the right to take ashore crockery, plates, cutlery, linen and other articles bearing the   165
Sellers' flag or name, provided they replace same with similar unmarked items. Library, forms, etc.,   166
exclusively for use in the Sellers' vessel(s), shall be excluded without compensation. Captain's,   167
Officers' and Crew's personal belongings including the slop chest are to be excluded from the sale,   168
as well as the following additional items (including items on hire):   169

The Buyers shall take over the remaining bunkers and unused lubricating oils in storage tanks and   170
sealed drums and pay the current net market price (excluding barging expenses) at the port and date   171
of delivery of the Vessel.   172
Payment under this Clause shall be made at the same time and place and in the same currency as   173
the Purchase Price.   174

8.   Documentation   175

The place of closing: 176

In exchange for payment of the Purchase Price the Sellers shall furnish the Buyers with delivery   177
documents, namely: 178

a)   Legal Bill of Sale in a form recordable in   (the country in which the Buyers are   179
        to register the Vessel), warranting that the Vessel is free from all encumbrances, mortgages   180
        and maritime liens or any other debts or claims whatsoever, duly notarially attested and   181
        legalized by the consul of such country or other competent authority.   182

b)   Current Certificate of Ownership issued by the competent authorities of the flag state of   183
        the Vessel.   184

c)   Confirmation of Class issued within 72 hours prior to delivery.   185

d)   Current Certificate issued by the competent authorities stating that the Vessel is free from   186
        registered encumbrances.   187

e)   Certificate of Deletion of the Vessel from the Vessel's registry or other official evidence of   188
        deletion appropriate to the Vessel's registry at the time of delivery, or, in the event that the   189
        registry does not as a matter of practice issue such documentation immediately, a written   190
        undertaking by the Sellers to effect deletion from the Vessel's registry forthwith and furnish a   191
        Certificate or other official evidence of deletion to the Buyers promptly and latest within 4   192
        (four) weeks after the Purchase Price has been paid and the Vessel has been delivered.   193

f)   Any such additional documents as may reasonably be required by the competent authorities   194
        for the purpose of registering the Vessel, provided the Buyers notify the Sellers of any such   195
        documents as soon as possible after the date of this Agreement.   196

At the time of delivery the Buyers and Sellers shall sign and deliver to each other a Protocol of   197
Delivery and Acceptance confirming the date and time of delivery of the Vessel from the Sellers to the   198
Buyers.   199

At the time of delivery the Sellers shall hand to the Buyers the classification certificate(s) as well as all   200
plans etc., which are on board the Vessel. Other certificates which are on board the Vessel shall also   201
be handed over to the Buyers unless the Sellers are required to retain same, in which case the   202
Buyers to have the right to take copies. Other technical documentation which may   203
be in the Sellers' possession shall be promptly forwarded to the Buyers at their expense, if they so   204
request. The Sellers may keep the Vessel's log books but the Buyers to have the right to take   205
copies of same.   206

9.   Encumbrances   207

The Sellers warrant that the Vessel, at the time of delivery, is free from all charters, encumbrances,   208
mortgages and maritime liens or any other debts whatsoever. The Sellers hereby undertake   209
to indemnify the Buyers against all consequences of claims made against the Vessel which have   210
been incurred prior to the time of delivery.   211

10.   Taxes, etc.   212

Any taxes, fees and expenses in connection with the purchase and registration under the Buyers' flag   213
shall be for the Buyers' account, whereas similar charges in connection with the closing of the Sellers'   214
register shall be for the Sellers' account.   215

11.   Condition on delivery   216

The Vessel with everything belonging to her shall be at the Sellers' risk and expense until she is   217
delivered to the Buyers, but subject to the terms and conditions of this Agreement she shall be   218
delivered and taken over as she was at the time of inspection, fair wear and tear excepted.   219
However, the Vessel shall be delivered with her class maintained without condition/recommendation*,   220
free of average damage affecting the Vessel's class, and with her classification certificates and   221
national certificates, as well as all other certificates the Vessel had at the time of inspection, valid and   222
unextended without condition/recommendation* by Class or the relevant authorities at the time of   223
delivery.   224
"Inspection" in this Clause 11, shall mean the Buyers' inspection according to Clause 4 a) or 4 b), if   225
applicable, or the Buyers' inspection prior to the signing of this Agreement. If the Vessel is taken over   226
without inspection, the date of this Agreement shall be the relevant date.   227

*   Notes, if any, in the surveyor's report which are accepted by the Classification Society   228
        without condition/recommendation are not to be taken into account.   229

12.   Name/markings   230

Upon delivery the Buyers undertake to change the name of the Vessel and alter funnel markings.   231

13.   Buyers' default   232

Should the deposit not be paid in accordance with Clause 2, the Sellers have the right to cancel this   233
Agreement, and they shall be entitled to claim compensation for their losses and for all expenses   234
incurred together with interest.   235
Should the Purchase Price not be paid in accordance with Clause 3, the Sellers have the right to   236
cancel the Agreement, in which case the deposit together with interest earned shall be released to the   237
Sellers. If the deposit does not cover their loss, the Sellers shall be entitled to claim further   238
compensation for their losses and for all expenses incurred together with interest.   239

14.   Sellers' default   240

Should the Sellers fail to give Notice of Readiness in accordance with Clause 5 a) or fail to be ready   241
to validly complete a legal transfer by the date stipulated in line 61 the Buyers shall have   242
the option of cancelling this Agreement provided always that the Sellers shall be granted a   243
maximum of 3 banking days after Notice of Readiness has been given to make arrangements   244
for the documentation set out in Clause 8. If after Notice of Readiness has been given but before   245
the Buyers have taken delivery, the Vessel ceases to be physically ready for delivery and is not   246
made physically ready again in every respect by the date stipulated in line 61 and new Notice of   247
Readiness given, the Buyers shall retain their option to cancel. In the event that the Buyers elect   248
to cancel this Agreement the deposit together with interest earned shall be released to them   249
immediately .   250
Should the Sellers fail to give Notice of Readiness by the date stipulated in line 61 or fail to be ready 251
to validly complete a legal transfer as aforesaid they shall make due compensation to the Buyers for   252
their loss and for all expenses together with interest if their failure is due to proven   253
negligence and whether or not the Buyers cancel this Agreement.   254

15.   Buyers' representatives   255

After this Agreement has been signed by both parties and the deposit has been lodged, the Buyers   256
have the right to place two representatives on board the Vessel at their sole risk and expense upon   257
arrival at   on or about   258
These representatives are on board for the purpose of familiarisation and in the capacity of   259
observers only, and they shall not interfere in any respect with the operation of the Vessel. The   260
Buyers' representatives shall sign the Sellers' letter of indemnity prior to their embarkation.   261

| 16. | **Arbitration** | 262 |

a)*   This Agreement shall be governed by and construed in accordance with English law and   263
any dispute arising out of this Agreement shall be referred to arbitration in London in   264
accordance with the Arbitration Acts 1950 and 1979 or any statutory modification or   265
re-enactment thereof for the time being in force, one arbitrator being appointed by each   266
party. On the receipt by one party of the nomination in writing of the other party's arbitrator,   267
that party shall appoint their arbitrator within fourteen days, failing which the decision of the   268
single arbitrator appointed shall apply. If two arbitrators properly appointed shall not agree   269
they shall appoint an umpire whose decision shall be final.   270

b)*   This Agreement shall be governed by and construed in accordance with Title 9 of the   271
United States Code and the Law of the State of New York and should any dispute arise out of   272
this Agreement, the matter in dispute shall be referred to three persons at New York, one to   273
be appointed by each of the parties hereto, and the third by the two so chosen; their   274
decision or that of any two of them shall be final, and for purpose of enforcing any award, this   275
Agreement may be made a rule of the Court.   276
The proceedings shall be conducted in accordance with the rules of the Society of Maritime   277
Arbitrators, Inc. New York.   278

c)*   Any dispute arising out of this Agreement shall be referred to arbitration at   279
, subject to the procedures applicable there.   280
The laws of   shall govern this Agreement.   281

*   *16 a), 16 b) and 16 c) are alternatives; delete whichever is not applicable. In the absence of*   282
deletions, alternative 16 a) to apply.   283

APPENDIX 2

BIMCO BULLETIN
VOLUME 89 NO. 2. 94
EXPLANATORY NOTES ON
SALEFORM 1993

EXPLANATORY NOTES FROM THE NORWEGIAN SHIPBROKERS ASSOCIATION TO THE SALEFORM 1993*

The Sale and Purchase Committee of the Norwegian shipbrokers Association in close cooperation with Nordisk Skibsrederforening (Northern Shipowners' Defence Club) and BIMCO, have been working for more than two years on a revision of the "Norwegian Saleform". A general modernisation of the document was required and the final version has been prepared after detailed study of the many comments submitted to the Committee during the hearing round, and subsequently.

The notes which follow are intended to highlight and clarify the more significant changes introduced in Saleform 1993.

The preamble now states that the Sellers and Buyers *have agreed to sell and ... buy* respectively.

A *Definitions* clause has now been introduced as part of the preamble.

CLAUSE 3—PAYMENT

The amendments *in every respect physically made ready for delivery and Notice of Readiness has been given in accordance with Clause 5* are directed at making it clear beyond doubt that the Sellers are not entitled to give notice of delivery before the Vessel is in every respect physically ready for delivery. These amendments were promoted by the English High Court judgement in the 'Aktion' which has been a source of some controversy in the market.

CLAUSE 4—INSPECTIONS

The Committee has chosen to provide for two alternatives, either a) outright sale after the Vessel and her class records have been inspected and accepted, or b) an inspection clause similar to that in Saleform 1987 except that 'afloat' has been deleted to take account of possible inspection of the Vessel in drydock.

CLAUSE 5—NOTICES, TIME AND PLACE OF DELIVERY

a. First a specific provision has been introduced for notices *of the estimated time of arrival at the intended place of drydocking/underwater inspection/delivery.*

 Secondly, the new wording placing emphasis on contractual readiness has been carried over from Clause 3, again with the 'Aktion' in mind.

b. The express requirement of safety of the place of delivery *is* new.

c. The prescribed mechanism by which Sellers can request extension of the cancelling date is new, although provisions of this type can be found in the cancelling clauses of certain voyage charter parties. It is certainly not the intention of this provision to enable Sellers to seek to extend time for illegitimate reasons. The underlying requirement of due diligence and the express right conferred on the Buyers to claim damages should guard against this.

---

* Reproduced by kind permission of the Baltic and International Maritime Council (BIMCO) and the Norwegian Shipbrokers Association.

d. The MoA now refers also to compromised total loss.

CLAUSE 6—A. DRYDOCKING B. DIVERS INSPECTION C. DRYDOCKING PROVISIONS

6a. and b. are alternatives. One is to be deleted from the outset.

it was previously very common for a 'diver clause' to be incorporated as an additional clause in the MoA. Clause 6 would then be deleted although the 'diver clause' would expressly relate back to the drydocking provisions contained in Clause 6! In so far as those provisions had by now formally been deleted, the Committee was advised that this gave rise to a legal conundrum. Further more by bringing a 'diver clause' into the main body of the MoA the Committee felt that it would be easier to spell out as clearly as possible the division of expenses in respect of both drydocking and diving operations and accompanying surveys.

As to the content of the clauses, having discussed the matter in some depth with BV, DNV, and Lloyd's Register, the Committee has decided to introduce several alterations. When the Vessel has been put in drydock the extent of the inspection by the classification societies have different inspection procedures of the classification society. The classification societies have different inspection procedures, however, thus whereas both Lloyd's and DNV manuals prescribe inspection form the deepest load line, BV provide for the whole of the outer shell to be inspected. The Committee thought it logical to adjust the description of the area to be inspected to below the deepest load line instead of 'Summer Load Line'.

The classification societies regard bottom inspection and tail shaft system inspection/survey as two independent and separate surveys. It is the intention that the bottom inspection will performed in accordance with class rules. However, if the tail shaft system is required to be surveyed by the classification surveyor, it is he who will decide upon the extent of that survey. He may, for example, require the simplex box and sealing rings to be checked in the case of oil leakage and not necessarily ask for the tail end shaft to be drawn. His findings are to take into account the current stage of the Vessel's survey cycle.

In clause 6 b. provision has been inserted to cover the situation as to time where, after an underwater inspection, class subsequently requires the Vessel to be put in drydock and no suitable drydocking facilities are available at the port of delivery. In such an event the cancelling date may be extended by a maximum of 14 days. Place of delivery after drydocking is intended to within the range in Clause 5 b. The Committee felt that it was desirable to prescribe a maximum period for extension of cancelling date. This should be kept well in mind when negotiating the date of cancelling.

Some classification societies now use the term 'condition' whereas BV, for example, still use 'recommendation'. hence the reference to 'condition/recommendation' in this Clause and Clause 11.

New provisions which have been included in Clause 6 c. (v) are the Buyers' right to have the Vessel's underwater parts cleaned and painted, and Sellers'' right to tender Notice of Readiness while the Vessel is in drydock in the event that the Buyers' work has not been completed by the time the Sellers have completed their work.

CLAUSE 7—SPARES/BUNKERS ETC.

Stores and provisions are now to be included in the sale without any extra payment in accordance with normal practice.

There is also now a provision for extra payment of unused lubricating oils in storage tanks and sealed drums.

CLAUSE 8—DOCUMENTATION

The provision for place of closing to be inserted is entirely new.

The documents listed as a. - e. reflect a minimum basic level of Sellers' obligations. With reference to item f. the Buyers may request additional documents required but the competent authorities for registration purposes, but the request is subject to the provisions of reasonableness and time.

CLAUSE 11—CONDITION ON DELIVERY

One of the reasons for the need to revise Saleform 1987 was the market's concern in relation to the changed provision contained in the second paragraph of Clause 11. The intention behind the change in 1983/87 was to make redundant the 'home made' additional 'clause 16' ie. the provision setting out the exceptions from the basic 'as is' principle. Unfortunately, the revised wording of Clause 11 gave rise to new and unforeseen problems, and the fact that the majority of contracts contained additional clauses maintaining the 'free of average damage' concept, only added to the confusion. While some uncertainties may now be resolved (see for examplethe 'Niobe' case currently going through the English courts) the Committee having considered in particular the comments form the hearing round has recommended that the new form incorporates the commonly used phrase free of average damage affecting the Vessel's class, coupled with the obligation to deliver the vessel with her class maintained without condition/recommendation. Finally, there is now an express provision dealing with certificates.

APPENDIX 3

NIPPONSALE 1993

| Issued 16 / 12 / 1965 |
| Amended 13 / 7 / 1971 |
| Amended 16 / 3 / 1977 |
| Amended 9 / 9 / 1993 |

The Documentary Committee of The Japan Shipping Exchange, Inc.

Copyright.
Published by
The Japan Shipping
Exchange, Inc.

MEMORANDUM OF AGREEMENT

Code Name : NIPPONSALE 1993

Date...

1   IT IS THIS DAY MUTUALLY AGREED between the Sellers mentioned in (i) below ("the Sellers")

2   and the Buyers mentioned in (ii) below ("the Buyers") that the Sellers shall sell and the Buyers

3   shall buy the Vessel named in (iii) below with particulars mentioned in (iv) - (viii) below ("the

4   Vessel"), which has been accepted by the Buyers as a result of their superficial inspection of the

5   Vessel at ....and examination of her Class Records, on the following

6   terms and conditions :

7   (i)   Sellers: ....

8   ....

9   (ii)   Buyers: ....

10   ....

11   (iii) Vessel's name: ....

12   (iv)   Flag: ....(v) Class: ....

13   (vi)   Built (year and builder's name): ....

14   (vii) Gross register tonnage: ....(viii) Summer dead-weight tonnage ....

15   1. PRICE

16   The Purchase Price of the Vessel shall be ....

17   ....

18   2. PAYMENT

19   (a) As security for the fulfilment of this Agreement, the Buyers shall pay a deposit of ten (10)

20   per cent of the Purchase Money to a bank nominated by the Sellers within three (3) banking

21   days from the date of this Agreement, in the names of the Sellers and the Buyers, which

22   shall be paid to the Sellers as a part of the Purchase Money in the same manner as the

23   ninety (90) per cent of the Purchase Money hereunder. Any interest earned on the deposit

24   shall be for the Buyers' account and any bank charges on the deposit shall be borne equally

25   by the Sellers and the Buyers.

26   (b) The Buyers shall remit the balance of the Purchase Money by telegraphic transfer to the

27   said bank immediately after the Notice of Readiness for Delivery is tendered by the Sellers

28   as per clause 7 of this Agreement. This balance shall be paid out to the Sellers together

29   with the said ten (10) per cent deposit against the Protocol of Delivery and Acceptance

30   being duly signed by the representatives of both parties at the time of delivery of the

31   Vessel.

32   3. DOCUMENTATION

33   At the time of delivery of the Vessel, the Sellers shall furnish the Buyers with the following

34   documents:

Reproduced by kind permission of the Japan Shipping Exchange, Inc.

35   (a) the Bill of Sale, duly attested by a Notary Public, specifying that the Vessel is free from all
36   debts, encumbrances and maritime liens,
37   (b) a letter from the Sellers undertaking to supply a Deletion Certificate from the
38   .... Registry promptly after the Vessel's delivery, and
39   (c) such other documents as may be mutually agreed.
40   Closing and exchange of documents shall take place at ....

41 **4. DELIVERY PLACE AND TIME**
42   (a) The Sellers shall deliver the Vessel to the Buyers at / in ....
43   .... not before ...., and not later than
44   .... ("the cancelling date").
45   (b) In the event the Sellers fail to make the Vessel ready for delivery on or before the cancelling
46   date, the Buyers shall have the option of maintaining or cancelling this Agreement,
47   provided such option shall be declared in writing within forty-eight (48) hours (Saturdays,
48   Sundays and Holidays excepted) from the cancelling date. However, any delay not
49   exceeding thirty (30) days caused by force majeure and/or by repairs in order to pass the
50   inspection under clause 6 of this Agreement shall be accepted by the Buyers.
51   (c) The Sellers shall keep the Buyers informed of the Vessel's itinerary and give the Buyers
52   thirty (30) / fifteen (15) / seven (7) / three (3) days notice of approximate expected place and
53   date of readiness for delivery.

54 **5. DELIVERY CONDITION**
55   The Sellers shall deliver to the Buyers the Vessel substantially in the same condition as when
56   the Vessel was inspected by the Buyers at the place mentioned in the preamble, fair wear and
57   tear excepted, but free from outstanding recommendations and average damage affecting her
58   present class with all her class, national and international trading certificates clean and valid at
59   the time of delivery.

60 **6. DRYDOCKING**
61   For the inspection by the Classification Society mentioned in (v) of the preamble of the Vessel's
62   bottom and other underwater parts below the summer load line ("bottom and other underwater
63   parts"), the Sellers shall place the Vessel in drydock at the port of delivery or near thereto prior
64   to delivery.
65   If the rudder, propeller, bottom or other underwater parts be found broken, damaged or
66   defective so as to affect the Vessel's clean certificate of class, the same shall be made good at
67   the Sellers' expense to the Classification Society's satisfaction so as to retain the Vessel's class
68   without qualification.
69   While the Vessel is in drydock and if required by the Buyers or the Classification Society's
70   surveyor, the tail-end shaft shall be drawn, and should the same be condemned or found
71   defective so as to affect the Vessel's clean certificate of class, it shall be renewed or made good
72   at the Sellers' expense to the Classification Society's satisfaction so as to retain the Vessel's
73   class without qualification.
74   The cost of drawing and replacing the tail-end shaft shall be borne by the Buyers unless the
75   Classification Society requires the tail-end shaft to be drawn, made good or renewed.
76   The expense of putting the Vessel in and taking her out of drydock and the drydock dues

77 including the fee of the Classification Society's surveyor shall be paid by the Buyers unless the
78 rudder, propeller, bottom, other underwater parts or tail-end shaft be found broken, damaged or
79 defective as aforesaid, in which event the Sellers shall pay these expenses.
80 The Sellers shall pay all costs of transporting the Vessel to the drydock and from the drydock to
81 the place of delivery.

82 7. NOTICE OF READINESS AND LIQUIDATED DAMAGES
83 When the Vessel has been approved by the Classification Society's surveyor following the
84 inspection stipulated in the preceding clause, the Vessel shall be deemed ready for delivery and
85 thereupon the Sellers shall tender to the Buyers a notice of readiness for delivery.
86 The Buyers shall take over the Vessel within three (3) banking days from the day of the receipt
87 of such notice inclusive.
88 In the event of the Buyers not taking delivery of the Vessel within the period specified above,
89 the Buyers shall pay to the Sellers the sum of .... per day as
90 liquidated damages, but such detention shall not exceed ten (10) days.

91 8. FORCE MAJEURE
92 Should the Vessel become an actual or constructive total loss before delivery or not be able to
93 be delivered through outbreak of war, political reasons, restraint of Governments, Princes or
94 People, or any other cause which either party hereto cannot prevent, this Agreement shall be
95 deemed to be null and void, and the deposit shall at once be returned in full to the Buyers.

96 9. ALLOCATION OF RISK
97 The Vessel with everything belonging to her shall be at the Sellers' risk and expense until she is
98 delivered to the Buyers, and after the delivery of the Vessel in accordance with this Agreement
99 the Sellers shall have no responsibility for any possible fault or deficiency of any description.

100 10. BELONGINGS AND BUNKERS
101 The Sellers shall deliver to the Buyers the Vessel with everything belonging to her at the time of
102 the superficial inspection mentioned in the preamble including all spare parts, stores and
103 equipment, on board or on shore, used or unused, except such things as are in the normal
104 course of operations used during the period between the superficial inspection and delivery.
105 Forwarding charges, if any, shall be for the Buyers' account.
106 The Buyers shall take over and pay the Sellers for remaining bunkers and unused lubricating
107 oils at last purchased prices evidenced by supporting vouchers. Payment under this clause shall
108 be made on or prior to delivery of the Vessel in the same currency as the Purchase Money.
109 The Sellers shall provide an inventory list for the Buyers at the time of delivery.

110 11. EXCLUSIONS FROM THE SALE
111 The Sellers have the right to take ashore crockery, plate, cutlery, linen and other articles bearing
112 the Sellers' flag or name, provided they substitute for the same an adequate number of similar
113 unmarked items. Books, cassettes and forms etc., exclusively for use on the Sellers' vessels,
114 shall be taken ashore before delivery.
115 Personal effects of the Master, Officers and Crew including slop chest, and hired equipment, if
116 any, are excluded from this sale and shall be removed by the Sellers prior to delivery of the

117   Vessel.

118   **12. CHANGE OF NAME ETC.**

119   The Buyers undertake to change the name of the Vessel and alter the funnel markings upon

120   delivery of the Vessel.

121   **13. ENCUMBRANCES ETC.**

122   The Sellers shall deliver to the Buyers the Vessel free from all debts, encumbrances and

123   maritime liens.

124   The Sellers hereby undertake to indemnify the Buyers against all consequences of claims made

125   against the Vessel in respect of liabilities incurred prior to the time of delivery.

126   **14. DEFAULT AND COMPENSATION**

127   Should the Buyers fail to fulfil this Agreement, the Sellers have the right to cancel the

128   Agreement, in which case the deposit shall be forfeited to the Sellers. If the deposit does not

129   cover the Sellers' loss caused by the Buyers' non-fulfilment of this Agreement, the Sellers shall

130   be entitled to claim further compensation from the Buyers for any loss and for all expenses.

131   If the Sellers should default in the delivery of the Vessel with everything belonging to her in the

132   manner and within the time herein specified, the deposit shall at once be returned to the Buyers

133   and in addition the Sellers shall, when such default is due to their negligent or intentional acts

134   or omissions, make due compensation for loss caused by their non-fulfilment of this Agreement.

135   **15. ARBITRATION**

136   Any dispute arising out of this Agreement shall be submitted to arbitration held in Tokyo by the

137   Tokyo Maritime Arbitration Commission ("TOMAC") of The Japan Shipping Exchange, Inc. in

138   accordance with the Rules of TOMAC and any amendments thereto, and the award given by the

139   arbitrators shall be final and binding on both parties.

The additional clauses from 16 to .... shall be deemed to be fully incorporated in this
Agreement.

IN WITNESS WHEREOF the Sellers and the Buyers have signed and executed TWO COPIES of this
Agreement the day and year first above written.

THE SELLERS   THE BUYERS

_____   _____

By :   By :
Title :   Title :

APPENDIX 4

THE BULLETIN OF THE
JAPAN SHIPPING EXCHANGE, INC.

NO. 27, DECEMBER 1993
NOTES ON NIPPONSALE 1993

Notes
on
MEMORANDUM OF AGREEMENT
for the sale and purchase of ships
Code Name: "NIPPONSALE 1993"

The Documentary Committee of the Japan Shipping Exchange, Inc. (Chairman : Yutaka Mizutani) officially adopted the draft of the revised MEMORANDUM OF AGREEMENT for the sale and purchase of ships, to be known as "NIPPONSALE 1993", at its general meeting in September 1993. The purpose of the revision is, generally, to update the "NIPPONSALE" form so as to reflect recent developments in practice in the sale and purchase of ships.

The main points of the revision are as follows:

1. **Titles are provided for each clause for users' convenience.**

2. **The Preamble makes clear the fact that the agreement is concluded after the Buyers accept the Vessel as a result of their superficial inspection of it.**
   This practice has been one of the most remarkable features of NIPPONSALE.

3. **The clause concerning the Government's Export and Import Licence, (former Clause 1.), is deleted.**
   These Licences used to be required for the sale and purchase of ships in many countries, but now they are not necessarily required. It should be considered the subject-matter of additional clauses which may be agreed between the parties.

4. **The clause for payment of a 10% deposit (former Clause 3.) and the clause for payment of the balance of the Purchase Money (former Clause 4.(a)) are dealt with in the same clause (Clause 2. PAYMENT) but in different paragraphs.**
   The characteristics of the two payments are different, i.e. while the 10% deposit should be paid immediately after the agreement is concluded as security for the fulfilment of the agreement, the balance of the Purchase Money should be remitted and paid with certainty after the Notice of Readiness for delivery. However, the manner and time of the two payments are, practically, often almost the same and in many cases the parties stipulate two simultaneous payments in an additional clause. Thus Clause 2. reflects

this practice for the users' convenience.

5. **The clause concerning establishing a Letter of Credit (former Clause 4.(b)) is deleted.**
In recent times Letters of Credit are not commonly used as a method of guarantee for payment.

6. **Concerning payment of the 10% deposit (Clause 2.(a)) and taking over the Vessel (Clause 7. NOTICE OF READINESS AND LIQUIDATED DAMAGES), in both cases the Buyers are now permitted three (3) banking days in which to perform: in the case of the deposit this must be paid within 3 banking days of the date of the Agreement, while taking over the Vessel must take place within 3 banking days of receipt of the above notice.**

7. **The clause concerning the physical condition of the Vessel at the time of delivery is newly stipulated in Clause 5. DELIVERY CONDITION.**

8. **The term "demurrage" in Clause 7. is replaced by "liquidated damages" because the former is properly an expression only applicable to describe certain liquidated damages arising in voyage charterparty situations and legally the latter is the proper wording for the purposes of this clause.**
However, as far as understanding by the business community is concerned, practically there is no change at all.

9. **The Sellers shall deliver the belongings of the Vessel to the Buyers without charge (Clause 10. BELONGINGS AND BUNKERS, 1st paragraph). But, the Buyers shall buy remaining bunkers and unused lubricating oils, at prices determined by reference to supporting vouchers (Clause 10. 2nd paragraph).**
This change reflects recent practice. Usually, the Sellers do not want to withdraw and forward the belongings of the Vessel considering the cost of doing so.
In practice, vouchers are used for deciding the prices of bunkers and lubricating oils because to determine the current market price at the port of delivery sometimes causes problems and takes time.

10. **The legal condition of the Vessel at the time of delivery is newly stipulated in Clause 13. ENCUMBRANCES ETC.**

11. **Clause 14. DEFAULT AND COMPENSATION makes it clear that the Sellers shall make due compensation when they default in the delivery of the Vessel within the**

time specified in the agreement due to their negligent or intentional acts or omissions, as well as returning the deposit.

NIPPONSALE 1993 is sold at the price of six hundred Japanese yen. It may be ordered by facsimile (Fax No. 81 3 3279 2785).
(The new form of "NIPPONSALE" is attached to the end of this Bulletin.)

APPENDIX 5

LONDON MARITIME ARBITRATORS' ASSOCIATION TERMS (1994)

THE L.M.A.A. TERMS (1994)

PRELIMINARY

1. These Terms may be referred to as "the L.M.A.A. Terms (1994)".

2. (a) In these Terms, unless the context otherwise requires,

    (i) "The Association" means the London Maritime Arbitrators' Association; "Member of the Association" includes both full and supporting members; "President" means the President for the time being of the Association

    (ii) "Tribunal" includes a sole arbitrator, a tribunal of two or more arbitrators, and an umpire

    (iii) "Original arbitrator" means an arbitrator appointed (whether initially or by substitution) by or at the request of a party as its nominee and any arbitrator duly appointed so to act following failure of a party to make its own nomination.

  (b) Save where original arbitrators, having disagreed, are thereafter requested and agree to act as advocates for presentation of the dispute to an umpire, an original arbitrator will at all times act with judicial impartiality and with exactly equal duties towards both parties and is in no sense to be considered as the representative of his appointer.

3. (a) The Terms apply to all arbitration proceedings commenced on and after 1st January 1994 whenever the dispute (unless it arises under an agreement providing for application to the arbitration of other specified rules or terms) is referred to members of the Association by their appointment as sole or original arbitrators and the dispute arises out of a transaction of a kind which, if it were to have been litigated in the High Court, would have been tried in the Admiralty or Commercial Courts. The Terms likewise apply whenever a sole or original arbitrator, not being a member, expressly accepts appointment on these Terms.

  (b) For the foregoing purpose arbitration proceedings shall be treated as having commmenced upon acceptance of appointment (i) by a sole arbitrator or (ii) whichever original arbitrator is first appointed.

JURISDICTION AND POWERS

4. (a) Subject to sub-paragraph (b) below, by submitting to arbitration under these Terms the parties confer upon the tribunal the jurisdiction and powers set out in the First Schedule.

  (b) A party shall be entitled to make application to the High Court, instead of to the tribunal, in relation to any interlocutory matters over which the High Court has jurisdiction; save that applications for security for costs shall be made to the High Court only with the concurrence of the other party or with leave of the tribunal.

TRIBUNAL'S FEES

5. Provisions regulating fees payable to the tribunal and other related matters are set out in the Second Schedule. Save as therein or herein otherwise provided, payment of the tribunal's fees and expenses is the joint and several responsibility of the parties.

ARBITRATION ON DOCUMENTS

6. If it is agreed that an arbitration is to be on documents (i.e. without an oral hearing) it is the responsibility of the parties to agree the procedure to be followed and to inform the tribunal of the agreement reached. The procedure set out in the Third Schedule should normally be adopted, with any such modifications as may be appropriate: and in default of agreement the tribunal will give appropriate directions.

7.   Applications for directions should not be necessary but, if required, they should be made in accordance with paragraph 10.

ORAL HEARINGS

8.   A time-table for preparation of the case for hearing should, whenever possible, be agreed between the parties and the tribunal should then be informed by the claimant of the agreement reached. In default of agreement, application for directions should be made in accordance with paragraph 10.

9.   (a)   A hearing date will not be fixed, save in exceptional circumstances, until the preparation of a case is sufficiently advanced to enable the duration of the hearing to be properly estimated; this will normally be after discovery has been completed.

   (b)   Unless the case calls for a preliminary meeting with the tribunal (see paragraph 11), it is the duty of the parties or their advisers, prior to application for a hearing date, to consult together (i) to assess the expected readiness and the likely duration of the hearing, (ii) to plan the preparatory work still to be done, and (iii) to consider whether any other directions are required from the tribunal when the hearing date is requested.

   (c)   Following such consultation, application for a hearing date must be made in writing, indicating the expected date of readiness and likely duration of the hearing.

   (d)   Following fixture of the hearing date a booking fee will be payable in accordance with the provisions of the Second Schedule.

INTERLOCUTORY APPLICATIONS

10.   (a)   Application to the tribunal for directions should, save in special circumstances, be made only after the other party has been afforded a reasonable opportunity to agree the terms of the directions proposed.

   (b)   If agreement is not reached, the applicant should apply to the tribunal, setting out the terms of the directions proposed. The application must be copied to the other party, who must respond to the tribunal (copy to the applicant) stating the grounds of objection. The response must be made within three working days, or such further time as the tribunal may allow on the application of the respondent party.

   (c)   Unless either party has requested an oral hearing, the tribunal will make its order following receipt of the response or, in default of response within the time allowed, upon expiry of that time.

   (d)   Prior to appointment of a third arbitrator, original arbitrators shall, if in agreement, be entitled to give directions without the need to appoint a third arbitrator for that purpose.

   (e)   Communications regarding interlocutory matters should be made expeditiously.

PRELIMINARY MEETINGS

11.   (a)   In cases where there are circumstances which merit preliminary informal discussion with the tribunal (including most cases involving a hearing of more than five days' duration) any application for a hearing should be preceded by a discussion between the parties' representatives to review the progress of the case; to reach agreement, so far as possible, upon further preparation for, and the conduct of, the hearing; to identify matters for discussion with the tribunal; and to prepare for submission to the tribunal an agenda of matters for approval or determination by it.

(b) Following the discussion between the parties' representatives, the parties should request a preliminary meeting with the tribunal, submitting their agenda together with an updated pleadings bundle and giving their estimates of readiness for hearing and the likely duration of the hearing.

(c) The preliminary meeting with the tribunal will be informal. Its object is to secure agreement so far as possible on the conduct of the arbitration generally, and to give any such directions as the tribunal considers fit.

(d) There is set out in the Fourth Schedule a guidance document indicating topics which may be appropriate for consideration prior to and, if still outstanding, at the preliminary meeting.

SETTLEMENT

12. It is the duty of the claimant (a) to notify the tribunal immediately if the arbitration is settled or otherwise terminated and (b) to inform the tribunal of the parties' agreement as to the manner in which payment will be made of any outstanding fees and expenses of the tribunal, e.g. for interlocutory work not covered by any booking fee paid.

13. Any booking fee paid will be dealt with in accordance with the provisions of paragraph (B) (1) (c) of the Second Schedule. Any other fees and expenses of the tribunal shall be settled, promptly and at latest within 28 days of presentation of the relevant account(s), in accordance with the agreement of the parties or, in default of agreement, the parties shall be jointly and severally responsible for such fees and expenses.

ADJOURNMENT

14. If a case is for any reason adjourned part-heard, the tribunal will be entitled to an interim payment, payable in equal shares or otherwise as the tribunal may direct, in respect of fees and expenses already incurred, appropriate credit being given for the booking fee.

15. The provisions of paragraph (B) (1) (d) of the Second Schedule shall apply in relation to adjournments ordered prior to the start of the hearing.

UMPIRES

16. An umpire who attends the principal hearing or any interlocutory application shall be entitled to remuneration accordingly for his services, irrespective of whether of not he is thereafter required to enter upon the reference, and as from the date of his appointment he shall, for the purposes of paragraphs 5 and 11 - 15 above, be treated as if he were a member of the tribunal.

AVAILABILITY OF ARBITRATORS

17. (a) In cases where it is known at the outset that an early hearing is essential, the parties should consult and ensure the availability of the arbitrator(s) to be appointed by them.

(b) If, in cases when the tribunal has already been constituted, the fixture of an acceptable hearing date is precluded by the commitments of the original appointee(s) the provisions of the Fifth Schedule shall apply.

THE AWARD

18. The time required for preparation of an award must vary with the circumstances of the case. The award should normally be available within not more than six weeks from the close of the proceedings. In many cases, and in particular where the matter is one of urgency, the interval should be substantially shorter.

19. The members of a tribunal need not meet together for the purpose of signing their award or of effecting any corrections thereto.

20. Where the reference is to a tribunal of three arbitrators, the majority view shall prevail in relation to any head of claim or counterclaim upon which unanimity is lacking. In the event of there being no majority the view of the third arbitrator shall prevail.

21. Unless a reasoned award is requested under Section 1 of the Arbitration Act 1979, the tribunal will normally supply the parties, on a confidential basis, with a document outlining the reasons for its decision. The document will not form part of the award, nor (unless the Court should otherwise direct) may it be relied upon or referred to by the parties in any proceedings relating to the award.

22. If any award has not been paid for and collected within one month of the date of publication, the tribunal may give written notice to either party requiring payment of the costs of the award whereupon such party shall be obliged to pay for and collect the award within fourteen days.

23. If, following the making of an interim award, outstanding matters are amicably resolved the tribunal should be promptly advised so that the file can be closed and documents disposed of.

24. If the tribunal considers that an arbitration decision merits publication then, provided such publication is not objected to by either or both of the parties, it may be published under such arrangements as the Association may effect from time to time. The publication will be so drafted as to preserve anonymity as regards the identity of the parties and of the tribunal.

GENERAL

25. Three months after publication of any final award the tribunal will notify the parties of its intention to dispose of the documents and to close the file, and it will act accordingly unless otherwise requested within 14 days of such notice being given.

26. In relation to any matters not expressly provided for herein the tribunal shall act in accordance with the tenor of these Terms.

THE FIRST SCHEDULE

(A) JURISDICTION

The tribunal shall have jurisdiction in relation to the following matters: —

(1)   To determine all disputes arising under or in connection with the transaction the subject of the reference, including (so far as the tribunal considers that course to be both practicable and desirable) any application for rectification of the contract and any further disputes arising subsequent to the commencement of the arbitration proceedings.

Provided however that, unless the parties otherwise agree, this jurisdiction shall not extend to determination of a dispute as to whether the transaction was the subject of an agreement binding in law upon the parties.

(2)   To proceed to an award on any claim or counterclaim on the application of the claimant party and without the need for an oral hearing if the respondent party (a) has failed to furnish defence submissions to such claim or counterclaim within such time as the tribunal has directed by final and peremptory order, and (b) (except where an arbitration on documents only has been agreed) has declined or failed to take advantage of an opportunity to apply to the tribunal for an oral hearing.

(3)   To impose, in relation to any final and peremptory order, such terms as the tribunal considers appropriate in the event of non-compliance with the order.

(4)   To make interim orders, upon the application of a respondent party to a claim or counterclaim, for the provision of security for that party's costs of the reference, with power to order a stay (either temporary or permanent) of the arbitration or to make such other direction as may in the circumstances be appropriate or if appropriate make an award dismissing the claim.

(5)   At the request of the parties or either of them or of its own volition, to correct any accidental mistake, omission, or error of calculation in its award, any such request to be made within 28 days of the collection of the award. Any correction may be effected in writing on the original award or in a separate memorandum which shall become part of the award.

(B) POWERS

Without derogation from all powers with which it is otherwise invested or with which it may be invested pursuant to application made to the High Court under Section 5(2) of the Arbitration Act 1979, the tribunal shall have the following specific powers, to be exercised as the circumstances may require for the most efficient and expeditious conduct of the reference:

(1)   To receive and act upon such oral or written evidence as it determines to be relevant, whether or not the evidence is strictly admissible in law.

(2)   To limit the number of expert witnesses, to direct that experts' reports be exchanged in advance of the hearing and, if the tribunal thinks fit, to direct that there be a "without prejudice" meeting of such experts within such period before or after the disclosure of the reports as the tribunal may direct, for the purpose of identifying those parts of their evidence which are at issue.

(3)   To direct, in appropriate circumstances, that statements of witnesses of fact be exchanged in advance of the hearing and be received as their evidence-in-chief.

(4)   To appoint, upon the application of any party, an expert assessor or assessors to sit with and advise the tribunal upon any matters which are outside its own expertise; the fees of any assessor(s) so appointed to form part of the cost of the award.

(5)   To direct, upon the application of any party or of its own volition, that anything the subject of the reference be made available for inspection by or on behalf of the tribunal or any party.

(6)   To require the parties to attend a preliminary meeting to deal with matters referred to in the fourth schedule or otherwise in the tribunal's discretion.

(C) MULTI-PARTY DISPUTES

A tribunal or tribunals shall have the following powers in relation to multi-party disputes:

(1)   To direct in appropriate cases that the references shall be heard concurrently and to give all such directions as to procedure as the interests of fairness, economy and expedition may require.

(2)   Upon the application of any party to an existing reference, the tribunal shall have power to direct that there be joined in that reference any other party or parties who, by written consent, have indicated readiness to be so joined; and the arbitration shall then proceed as though the tribunal had been appointed to deal with all associated disputes between the respective interests on a consolidated basis.

THE SECOND SCHEDULE

TRIBUNAL'S FEES

(A) Appointment fee

An appointment fee is payable on appointment by the appointing party or by the party at whose request the appointment is made. The appointment fee shall be a standard fee fixed by the Committee of the Association from time to time. Unless otherwise agreed, the appointment fee of an umpire or third arbitrator shall in the first instance be paid by the claimant.

(B) Booking fee

(1) (a) For a hearing of up to ten days' duration there shall be payable to the tribunal a booking fee of £250 per person or such sum as the Committee of the Association may from time to time decide, for each day reserved. The booking fee will be invoiced to the party asking for the hearing date to be fixed or to the parties in equal shares if both parties ask for the hearing date to be fixed as the case may be and shall be paid within 14 days of confirmation of the reservation or six months in advance of the first day reserved ("the start date"), whichever date be the later. If the fee is not paid in full by the due date the tribunal will be entitled to cancel the reservation but either party may secure reinstatement of the reservation by payment within seven days of any balance outstanding.

      (b) For hearings over ten days duration the booking fee in sub-paragraph (1)(a) above shall for each day reserved be increased by 30% in the case of a hearing of up to 15 days and 60% in the case of a hearing up to 20 days and may, at the discretion of the tribunal, be subscribed in non-returnable stage payments. For hearings in excess of 20 days the booking fee to be at the rate for a hearing of 20 days plus such additional sum as may be agreed between the parties in the light of the length of the proposed hearing.

      (c) Where the case proceeds to an award, or is settled subsequent to the start of the hearing, appropriate credit will be given for the booking fee in calculating the cost of the award or, as the case may be, the amount payable to the tribunal upon settlement of the case.

      (d) Where a hearing date is vacated prior to the start date the booking fee will be retained by the tribunal (i) in full if the date is vacated less than three months before the start date (ii) as to 50% if the date is vacated three months or more before the start date. Any interlocutory fees and expenses incurred will also be payable or, as the case may be, deductible from the refund under (ii).

(2) An arbitrator or umpire who, following receipt of his booking fee or any part thereof, is for any reason replaced is, upon settlement of his fees for any interlocutory work, responsible for transfer of his booking fee to the person appointed to act in his place. In the event of death the personal representatives shall have a corresponding responsibility.

ACCOMMODATION

(1) If accommodation and/or catering is arranged by the tribunal, the cost will normally be recovered as part of the cost of the award, but where a case is adjourned part-heard or in other special circumstances, the tribunal reserves the right to direct that the cost shall be provisionally paid by the parties in equal shares (or as the tribunal may direct) promptly upon issue of the relevant account. Prior to booking accommodation and/or catering the tribunal may, if they think fit, request that they be provided with security sufficient to cover their prospective liabilities in respect thereof.

(2) If accommodation is reserved and paid for by the parties and it is desired that the cost incurred be the subject of directions in the award, the information necessary for that purpose must be furnished promptly to the tribunal.

THE THIRD SCHEDULE

ARBITRATION ON DOCUMENTS

RECOMMENDED PROCEDURE

If parties wish a dispute to be decided without an oral hearing the procedure set out in paragraphs 1 - 5 below is recommended for adoption by agreement.

When this procedure (or any modification) has been agreed, the tribunal should be so informed. The tribunal must be promptly advised if, at a later stage, the parties or either of them consider that an oral hearing is going to be necessary.

The exchange of submissions, etc., will take place directly between the parties unless the case is being handled by others (e.g. by lawyers or a Club) on their behalf.

Copies of all submissions, comments and documents must be supplied simultaneously to the tribunal, and all communications with the tribunal must be copied to the other party.

All documents relied on must be legibly copied and translations supplied as necessary.

---

(1) Claimants' written submissions, together with copies of supporting documents, to be furnished by them within 28 days after the agreement by the parties to adopt the procedure.

(2) Respondents' written submissions (including those relating to any counterclaim), together with copies of any documents relied on additional to those already provided by the claimants, to be furnished by them within 28 days after receipt of the claimants' submissions and documents.

(3) If there is no counterclaim, claimants' final comments (if any) onthe claim to be furnished within 21 days after receipt of the respondents' submissions and documents.

(4) If there is a counterclaim:
   (a) claimants to furnish comments and any additional documents relative to the counterclaim within 28 days after receipt of the respondents' submissions and documents;
   (b) respondents' final comments (if any) on the counterclaim to be furnished within 21 days after receipt of the claimants' comments and additional documents (if any).

(5) The tribunal will then give notice to the parties of its intention to proceed to its award and will so proceed unless either party within seven days requests, and is thereafter granted, leave to provide further submissions and/or documents.

THE FOURTH SCHEDULE
PRELIMINARY MEETINGS

Paragraph 11 of the Terms envisages that where the hearing of a case is expected to last more than five days, or if there are other special circumstances, the representatives should first review the progress of the matter and consider preparations for the hearing, and thereafter a preliminary meeting should take place with the tribunal to consider those matters (see paragraph 11 of the Terms for fuller details).

This Schedule sets out, in check-list form, topics which may be appropriate for consideration. The representatives' discussion should lead to a measure of procedural agreement, and any remaining areas for discussion with the tribunal can be identified and the scope for specific directions from the tribunal thus reduced.

In complex cases, more than one preliminary meeting may be required in order to deal with developments since, or any matters stood over at, a prior meeting.

Because cases vary so much, the procedure and matters for consideration must be flexible. Inevitably, certain matters must be left to the discretion of the parties' advisers (e.g. what facts can be agreed, how evidence is to be dealt with, what level of representation is required, etc.); those mentioned in the check-list are not, in all instances, matters on which the tribunal can or will rule. This makes it all the more important that the representatives first consider in a comprehensive, realistic and co-operative way all the relevant points listed, always bearing in mind the underlying object of the anticipated meetings: to achieve the speediest, cheapest and most efficient resolution of the parties' disputes.

1. Pleadings
    (i)   closed (including particulars)?
    (ii)   amendments required?
    (iii) are all issues still alive?

2. Discovery
    (i)   completed?
    (ii)   disputes re outstanding discovery.

3. The Hearing
    A. General
    (i)   preliminary issues appropriate for determination? (e.g. interpretation of contract, liability only, etc.)
    (ii)   any issues suitable for determination on written submissions alone?

    B. Evidence (Fact)
    (i)   can some facts/figures be agreed?
    (ii)   exchange lists of witnesses of fact (indicating broadly areas each will deal with?
    (iii) presentation of some evidence-in-chief by proofs or affidavits appropriate? If so, what arrangements should be made re exchange prior to hearing?
    (iv)   admission of some evidence (perhaps formal or of marginal importance) in proof or affidavit form only?

    C. Evidence (Expert)
    (i)   expert(s) needed? If so, should numbers be limited, generally or by reference to specific aspects of dispute?
    (ii)   when should reports be exchanged (leaving enough time for reply reports to be supplied well before hearing)?
    (iii) should a "without prejudice meeting" of experts be held?
    (iv)   could tribunal deal with technical aspects on basis of reports, without need to call experts?
    (v)   could an independent assessor usefully assist tribunal?

D. Inspection

would tribunal be assisted by attending trials or experiments, or inspecting any object featuring in the dispute?

E. Documents

(i)   if possible provide agreed chronology, dramatis personae, list of telex answerbacks, agreed statement of accounts.

(ii)   arrangements of documents (e.g. different bundles for different topics, or as appropriate) and dates by which bundles to be produced.

(iii)   unnecessary inclusion of documents to be avoided.

(iv)   when documents voluminous, consider copying only key bundles, holding other material available for reference and copying if required.

F. Advance Reading

(i)   provision of pleadings and other suitable material (e.g. experts' reports) to tribunal as far in advance of hearing as possible.

(ii)   should time be set aside during hearing, after appropriate opening, for private reading of any documents by tribunal (to reduce time otherwise involved in reading documents out)?

G. Multi-Party Disputes

(i)   procedure generally.

(ii)   consolidated, concurrent or consecutive hearings?

H. Representation

level of representation at hearing appropriate to case.

4. Hearing Dates

(The fixing of dates will, in the majority of cases, be most usefully considered after the matters covered in paragraph 3 have been reviewed, for they are bound to have a considerable bearing on how long the hearing is likely to take, and when the parties can be ready.)

(i)   estimated duration of hearing.

(ii)   when can parties realistically be expected to be ready?

(iii)   any problems re availability of witnesses? (If so, can these be mitigated by taking evidence in advance, or using proofs/affidavits?)

(iv)   availability of tribunal (see LMAA Terms, paragraph 17 and Fifth Schedule).

(v)   accommodation required and numbers attending.

(vi)   any special facilities required (e.g. transcripts, interpreters, etc.).

(vii)   arrangements for accommodation, etc.: who to book/pay for?

THE FIFTH SCHEDULE

RECONSTITUTION OF THE TRIBUNAL

The following provisions are directed to avoiding delay which the parties or either of them consider unacceptable, but if both parties prefer to retain a tribunal as already constituted they remain free so to agree.

(1)   The governing factor will be the ability of the tribunal to fix a hearing date within a reasonable time of the expected readiness date as notified by the parties on application for a date (see paragraph 9 (c) of the Terms), or, if they are not agreed as to the expected readiness date, within a reasonable time of whichever forecast date the tribunal considers more realistic.

(2)   For hearings of up to 10 days estimated duration, what constitutes a reasonable time will (unless the parties apply for a date further ahead) be determined by reference to the estimated length of hearing as follows: —

ESTIMATED DURATION	REASONABLE TIME
(i) Up to 2 days	3 months
(ii) 3 - 5 days	6 months
(iii) 6 - 10 days	10 months

"Relevant time-scale" is used below to mean whichever of the foregoing periods is applicable and, in cases of more than 10 days duration, such corresponding time-scale as the tribunal may consider appropriate.

(3)   A sole arbitrator who is unable to offer a date within the relevant time-scale will offer to retire and, if so requested by the parties or either of them, will retire upon being satisfied that an appropriate substitute appointment has been effected by the parties; in event of their disagreement, either party may request the President to make the necessary substitute appointment.

(4)   In all other cases, unless all members of the tribunal are able to offer a matching date within the relevant time-scale:

(A)   the tribunal will have regard to any agreed preference of the parties, but if there is no agreed preference the tribunal will fix:

(i)   the earliest hearing date that can be given by any member(s) able to offer a guaranteed date within the relevant time-scale;

    or

(ii)   if a guaranteed date within the relevant time-scale cannot be offered by any member of the tribunal, the earliest date thereafter which can be guaranteed by any member(s) of the tribunal;

on the basis, in either case, that any member then unable (by reason of a prior commitment) to guarantee the date so fixed will (unless that prior commitment has meanwhile cleared) retire by notice given six clear weeks prior to the start date.

(B)   Upon notification of any such retirement an appropriate substitution will be effected as follows: —

(i)   If an original arbitrator retires the substitute shall be promptly appointed by his appointer; or failing such appointment at least 21 days prior to the start date the substitute will then be appointed by the umpire or third arbitrator or, if an umpire or third arbitrator has not yet been appointed, the substitute will be appointed by the President;

(ii)   If an umpire or third arbitrator retires the substitute will be appointed by the original arbitrators.

(5) For the purpose of paragraph (4):

  (A) "Appropriate substitution" means appointment of a substitute able to match the hearing date established in accordance with sub-paragraph (A)

  (B) "Start date" means the first date reserved for the hearing

  (C) An umpire or third arbitrator will retain power to make any necessary substitution under sub-paragraph (B) (i) notwithstanding that he may himself have given notice of retirement under sub-paragraph (A) and an original arbitrator will retain the like power under sub-paragraph (B) (ii).

(6) Applications to vacate dates fixed by implementation of this Schedule will be granted only in exceptional circumstances. The convenience of counsel and/or expert witnesses will not normally be treated as justifying vacation of the date.

Printed by Cravitz Printing Company Limited, 1 Tower Hill, Brentwood, Essex CM14 4TA.

APPENDIX 6

NOTES ON LMAA TERMS (1994)
AND
RECOMMENDED ARBITRATION CLAUSE

NOTES ON THE L.M.A.A. TERMS (1994)

Introduction

1987 saw the introduction of these new Terms. They were slightly revised in 1991 to give effect to changes found to be necessary as a result of experience in their use. A further reconsideration of the Terms during 1993 has resulted in a number of additional changes. Although none of the changes to the Terms are radical, to avoid confusion it has been decided to re-designate them as the L.M.A.A. Terms (1994).

The ambit of the terms under which the Association's members operated until 1987 was relatively restricted. The 1987 Terms were prompted by a growing feeling that it would be helpful to all concerned — and in line with the practice of other arbitral organisations — if a more comprehensive set of ground-rules were to be established.

The Terms are the fruit of a process of continuing consultation. It is *not* the intention to "institutionalise" L.M.A.A. arbitrations, but simply to provide in a clear and convenient form guidelines aimed at making for greater efficiency and despatch in the conduct of the arbitration.

The 1984 Terms will normally apply to arbitrations started before 1st January 1987, the unrevised 1987 Terms to arbitrations started between 1st January 1987 and 31st March 1991 and the revised 1987 Terms to arbitrations started between 1st April 1991 and 31st December 1993. The 1994 Terms apply to arbitrations commenced on or after 1st January 1994, but can be applied by agreement to arbitrations commenced before that date.

Content of the Terms

The main body of the document provides the general framework and is largely self-explanatory. It supplies general guidance as to procedure at the various stages of the arbitration and deals with other matters of an administrative nature.

The five Schedules cover a number of self-contained topics. The following will give a general indication of their content and purpose.

First Schedule — Jurisdiction and Powers

Attention is drawn, in particular, to the tribunal's jurisdiction to deal with security for costs; to relaxation of the strict rules of evidence; to the admission of witness' statements as evidence-in-chief; and to the encouragement of co-operation between expert witnesses. These are, in the main, provisions aimed at saving time and expense.

Second Schedule — Tribunal's Fees

The booking fee arrangements which were introduced in the 1984 Terms have been modified in a number of important respects. They were further altered by the 1991 revision and are extended in the 1994 Terms to cover the longer hearings. For appointments prior to 1st April 1991 the fee will normally be payable by the parties in equal shares. As from that date the fee will be invoiced to the party asking for the hearing or to the parties in equal shares if both parties ask for a date. It will be partially returnable if the hearing date is vacated at least three monthe before the first day fixed for the hearing. Moreover, no booking fee will be payable until six months in advance of the hearing date. For appointments on and after 1st April 1991 the tribunal may request security to cover their prospective liabilities for accommodation and/or catering prior to booking the same.

The Association is satisfied that a booking fee system is, under modern conditions, essential in the interests of parties and arbitrators alike; and it is believed that the system that has been established will be seen as fair and equitable.

Third Schedule — Arbitration on Documents

This replaces the old "Short Form Rules" and provides, in effect, a procedural model for employment in "documents only" cases.

Fourth Schedule — Preliminary Meetings

The check-list contained in the Schedule is designed to assist the parties and the tribunal in considering how the case can best be prepared for presentation at the hearing — the declared aim being "to achieve the speediest, cheapest and most efficient resolution of the parties' disputes".

Encouragement of the parties to get to grips with cases in advance may, it is hoped, lead to narrowing of the issues and, in some cases, to a settlement being reached before expense is incurred in the final run-up to the hearing.

Fifth Schedule — Reconstitution of the Tribunal

A comprehensive set of rules is provided which ensures that the parties secure a hearing within a reasonable time of application for a hearing date.

It will be noted that there are safeguards to deal with any case in which obstruction might be encountered; but it is hoped that parties and their advisers will willingly co-operate to eliminate a source of complaint which, in the past, was often justified.

Applicability of the Terms

Paragraph 3 of the Terms sets out the circumstances in which their previous provisions will be automatically operative.

There can however, be no objection to the Terms being adopted, by agreement, by arbitrators who are not members of the L.M.A.A., and the last sentence of paragraph 3(a) is designed positively to encourage that practice.

Arbitration Clause

The parties may wish to consider the use of an arbitration clause which expressly provides for the proceedings to be subject to the L.M.A.A. Terms.

A suggested form of clause is set out overleaf. It provides for the constitution of a tribunal if the parties do not agree upon a sole arbitrator. The clause can readily be modified if the preference should be for a tribunal composed of two arbitrators, with power to appoint an umpire if they disagree.

Agreement upon a sole arbitrator has obvious economic attractions, particularly in the case of arbitrations on documents or where the amount at stake is modest.

It would be in the parties' interest normally to appoint persons who are UK-resident and thus readily available to participate in an arbitration to be held in London.

L.M.A.A. ARBITRATION CLAUSE

All disputes or differences arising out of or under this cotract which cannot be amicably resolved shall be referred to arbitration in London.

Unless the parties agree upon a sole arbitrator, one arbitrator shall be appointed by each party. In the case of an arbitration on documents, if the two arbitrators so appointed are in agreement their decision shall be final. In all other cases the arbitrators so appointed shall appoint a third arbitrator and the reference shall be to the three-man tribunal thus constituted.

If either of the appointed arbitrators refuses to act or is incapable of acting, the party who appointed him shall appoint a new arbitrator in his place.

If one party fails to appoint an arbitrator, whether originally or by way of substitution for two weeks after the other party, having appointed his arbitrator, has (by telex, fax or letter) called upon the defaulting party to make the appointment, the President for the time being of the London Maritime Arbitrators' Association shall, upon application of the other party, appoint an arbitrator on behalf of the defaulting party and that arbitrator shall have the like powers to act in the reference and make an award (and, if the case so requires, the like duty in relation to the appointment of a third arbitrator) as if he had been appointed in accordance with the terms of the agreement.

This contract is governed by English law and there shall apply to all proceedings under this clause the Terms of the London Maritime Arbitrators Association current at the time when the arbitration proceedings were commenced. All appointees shall be members of the Association.

Provided that where the amount in dispute does not exceed the sum of US $50,000 (or such other sum as the parties may agree) any dispute shall be resolved in accordance with the Small Claims Procedure of the London Maritime Arbitrators' Association.

APPENDIX 7

BILL OF SALE IN
BRITISH FORM ROS 20 1/94

Department of Transport
Merchant Shipping (Registration, etc.) Act 1993

BILL OF SALE

* R O S 2 0 *

* **Warning:** A purchaser of a British registered ship does not obtain a complete title until the appropriate Bill(s) of Sale has been recorded with the Registry, and a new Certificate issued.
* Registered owners or mortgagees *must* inform the Registry of any change of address.
* Where one owner is selling to two or more owners, separate forms are required unless they are buying as joint owners.
* Unless application to transfer the registration of the vessel to the new ownership is received at the Registry within 30 days of the change, re-registration fees will be payable.
* Please write in black ink using BLOCK CAPITALS, and tick boxes where appropriate.

SECTION 1: DETAILS OF THE SHIP

NAME OF SHIP

OFFICIAL NUMBER (if any)   LENGTH (metres)

SECTION 2: DETAILS OF THE SALE

Body Corporate please give	Company name	Principal Place of Business #	
Individuals please give	Full name(s)	Address(es)	Occupation(s)
*I/we the transferor(s) ☐ as joint owners *(Please tick box if you are joint owners)*			

in consideration of (*the sum of)

*paid/given to *me/us by:

Body Corporate please give	Company name	Principal Place of Business #	
Individuals please give	Full name(s)	Address(es)	Occupation(s)
the transferee(s) ☐ as joint owners *(Please tick box if you are joint owners)*			

Companies incorporated other than in the UK or British Dependent Territories - enter place of business   ***Delete as necessary**

ROS 20 1/94

Crown copyright is reproduced with the permission of the Controller of HMSO.

SECTION 2: DETAILS OF SALE (continued)

the receipt of which is acknowledged, transfer
shares in the above ship and in its appurtenances to the transferee(s).

(figures and words)

Further, *I/we the said transferor(s) for *myself/ourselves, hereby declare that *I/we have the power to transfer in the manner aforesaid the above-mentioned shares, and that they are free from encumbrances.

If any registered mortgage is outstanding, please tick the following box:

"save as appears by the registry of the above ship"

SECTION 3: FOR COMPLETION WHEN SALE IS BY A COMPANY

Executed by the transferor as a deed on this   *COMPANY SEAL*

          day of   **19**   **by:-**

* (a)   **the affixing of the common seal of the transferor
         in the presence of the following persons signing;** *or*
* (b)   **signing by the following persons;**

Director _____

Director/Secretary _____

Authorised Signatory _____   Authorised Signatory _____

NOTE: IN SCOTLAND - signature may be by: *EXCEPT IN SCOTLAND - signature may be by:*
       two directors; **or**   *two directors;* **or**
       by a director and the secretary of the company; **or**   *by a director and the secretary of the company. If the*
       by any two persons authorised to sign and subscribe   *common seal is affixed, any special requirements of the*
       the documents on behalf of the company.   *company's articles about signing must be complied with.*

SECTION 4: FOR COMPLETION WHEN SALE IS BY INDIVIDUAL(S)

* **Executed as a deed** (in England or Wales)   Seal if
* **Signed** (in Scotland)   executed in
* **Signed, sealed and delivered** (in Northern Ireland)   Northern
                                                                  Ireland

   on this _____ **day of** _____ **19** _____
   by the following person(s) signing as transferor(s)

Signature(s) of transferor(s)		
Full name of witness(es)		
Signature of witness(es)		
Occupation of witness(es)		
Address of witness(es)		

       NOTE: In Scotland, two witnesses are required; elsewhere, one witness.

                                                              * Delete as necessary

When completed you should send this form, together with the appropriate fee and supporting documents (if required) to: REGISTRY OF SHIPPING AND SEAMEN PO BOX 165, CARDIFF, CF4 5FU.	OFFICIAL USE ONLY Entry in Register made on _____ (date) at _____ (time) Officer's initials _____

APPENDIX 8

REGIONAL PORT STATE
CONTROL AGREEMENTS

Appendix 8—Regional
Port State Control Agreements

1. **Paris Memorandum of Understanding**

Belgium	Italy
Canada	Netherlands
Denmark	Norway
Finland	Poland
France	Portugal
Germany	Spain
Greece	Sweden
Ireland	United Kingdom
Italy	

2. **Viña del Mar Agreement**

Argentina	Panama
Brazil	Peru
Chile	Uruguay
Colombia	Venezuela
Mexico	

3. **Tokyo Memorandum of Understanding**

Australia	Malaysia
Canada	New Zealand
China	Papua New Guinea
Fiji	Philippines
Hong Kong	Russia
Indonesia	Singapore
Japan	Solomon Islands

Index